∞

The Basic Book of
Catholic Prayer

Also available
from Sophia Institute Press®
by the Reverend Lawrence G. Lovasik:

The Hidden Power of Kindness:
A Practical Handbook for Souls Who
Dare to Transform the World,
One Deed at a Time

The Basic Book of Catholic Prayer

How to Pray and Why

by the Reverend
Lawrence G. Lovasik

SOPHIA INSTITUTE PRESS®
Manchester, New Hampshire

The Basic Book of Catholic Prayer: How to Pray and Why is an abridged version of *Prayer in Catholic Life* (New York: The Macmillan Company, 1961) and contains editorial revisions to the original text.

Printed in the United States of America.

Cover design: Coronation Media in collaboration with Perceptions Design Studios.

On the cover: Knelt in Prayer, Absolon, John (1815-95) / Private Collection / Photo © Peter Nahum at The Leicester Galleries, London / The Bridgeman Art Library.

Sophia Institute Press
Box 5284, Manchester, NH 03108
1-800-888-9344
www.SophiaInstitute.com
Sophia Institute Press® is a registered trademark of Sophia Institute.

Imprimi potest: Raymond J. Weisenberger, S.V.D.,
Provincial, Girard, Pennsylvania
Nihil obstat: Rt. Rev. Msgr. Wilfrid J. Nash, Litt.D., Censor
Imprimatur: John Mark Gannon, D.D., D.C.L., LL.D.,
Archbishop of Erie, September 29, 1958

Library of Congress Cataloging-in-Publication Data
Lovasik, Lawrence G. (Lawrence George), 1913-
    [Prayer in Catholic life]
    The basic book of Catholic prayer : how to pray and why / Lawrence G. Lovasik.
       p. cm.
    Originally published: Prayer in Catholic life. New York : Macmillan, 1961.
    Includes bibliographical references.
    ISBN 1-928832-04-0 (pbk. : alk. paper)
    1. Prayer — Catholic Church. 2. Catholic Church — Doctrines. I. Title.
BV210.2.L65 1999
248.3'2 — dc21   99-057341

∞

Contents

Part One
Develop an
understanding of prayer

Part Two
Practice the forms of prayer

∞

Foreword

You cannot progress steadily toward the goal of life — to know, love, and serve God — without a willed dependence on God at each stage of that progress. Prayer is the expression of that willed dependence. It is, therefore, an essential means to salvation. If prayer is wanting, all other means are of no avail. Hence, it is most important that everyone has a clear and accurate notion of what real prayer is.

Our Lord told us to "pray always,"[1] and we cannot fulfill this obligation unless we have learned the art of praying rightly. St. Augustine[2] once said, "He knows how to live well who knows how to pray well." And St. Vincent de Paul's[3] conviction was:

---

[1] Cf. Luke 18:1. The biblical quotations in these pages are based on the Douay-Rheims edition of the Old and New Testaments except where they are based on the Revised Standard Version, indicated by the following symbol: (RSV). Where applicable, biblical quotations have been cross-referenced with the differing names and numeration in the Revised Standard Version, using the following symbol: (RSV =). — ED.

[2] St. Augustine (354-430), Bishop of Hippo.

[3] St. Vincent de Paul (c. 1580-1660), founder of the Lazarist Fathers and the Sisters of Charity.

"There is certainly nothing more useful than prayer. This is why we should esteem it, love it much, and neglect nothing in order to do it well."

The purpose of this book is to encourage you to set about acquiring the art of praying, by equipping you with accurate notions of the nature, the role, and the subject of prayer.

May the Immaculate Heart of Mary, the Singular Vessel of Devotion, of whom St. Luke says, "Mary kept all these words, pondering them in her heart,"[4] teach us how to pray!

Reverend Lawrence G. Lovasik

[4] Luke 2:19.

∞

The Basic Book of
Catholic Prayer

Part One

∞

Develop
an understanding
of prayer

Chapter One

∞

Understand what prayer is

Prayer is the lifting up of our minds and hearts to God, to praise His goodness, to thank Him for His kindness, to acknowledge our sins and plead for pardon, to ask His aid for our salvation, and to give glory to Him.

Note the words *mind and heart*. Not every thought of God is a prayer. A person may spend hours thinking of God and yet not be praying. When you pray, your mind and your heart or your will are active: your mind occupies itself in thinking of God and your relation to Him; your heart or your will performs acts of worship. Your mind and your heart are, so to speak, two wings by which your soul lifts itself to God. The skylark soars high into the heavens, where it sings its beautiful songs. So, too, when you pray, your mind and heart soar heavenward; you think devoutly of God and you speak devoutly to God.

While entertaining a friend, you forget everything else. When you pray, you ought also to forget earthly things; your heart should speak only to God. "Prayer is conversation with God." Thus wrote St. Clement of Alexandria[5] in the second

---

[5] St. Clement of Alexandria (c. 150-c. 215), theologian.

century. Aware of God, looking at Him with the eyes of your soul, you reach toward Him to converse with Him, to give Him what you have, to make your will one with His. You adore, praise, and thank Him. You ask for His help and His pardon. You trust God in the simplest way, confiding to Him all that you have most at heart — your sorrows and joys, your hopes and fears, your desires and plans. In return, you receive from Him help, consolation, and advice.

You speak quite plainly with God of the most important matters and often without any feeling or emotion. All that matters is that you speak honestly and earnestly. You pray well when you tell God what is in your heart. Thus, prayer is communication of spirit with spirit, of man with God.

St. Francis de Sales[6] says, "The chief exercise of prayer is to speak to God and to hear God speak in the bottom of your heart." So, talk to God as simply and naturally as you talk to your mother. Be ever conscious that His love of you surpasses even hers; that to Him you owe all you have; that your whole happiness depends on His kindness and generosity; and that, since He is truly your Father, He desires to have you tell Him whatever is on your mind and in your heart.

Prayer is the simplest and most natural expression of worship. All intelligent creatures are bound to think about God and to converse with Him — in other words, to pray to Him. Prayer requires no learning or eloquence. In order to pray, you need only to understand who God is and who you are; you need only to understand how great is God's fatherly goodness and how deep your own misery. Faith will teach you all that is

---

[6] St. Francis de Sales (1567-1622), Bishop of Geneva.

necessary. But your prayer, to be true prayer, must be from your heart.

You can pray to God at any time and in any place, for you are always in His presence. His love for you is always the same. Even when you are swamped with worldly cares and selfish interests, He is close to you; you will always find Him waiting to listen, ready to answer.

God is the source of all peace and joy. Prayer unites us with God. Hence, you cannot find a better means of relaxing your body and mind than by lifting up your mind and heart to God in prayer.

∽

Through prayer, you communicate with God

It is an indescribable grace and honor to have God listen to you and allow you to seek His presence. Nowhere are you received so sincerely and so lovingly. Try to appreciate the great privilege of being able to talk with God.

Many people imagine that they are doing ever so much for the Lord when they pray. That is foolish conceit. God does not need our prayers, but we need God and His grace.

If a person has received permission to appear before our Holy Father the Pope, we say that the person has been granted an audience. Everyone regards that as a great favor and honor. When you pray, you are permitted to speak to God; He grants you an audience. Should you not often take advantage of that special favor and honor? You are permitted to go to God at any hour of the day or night; He is always ready to receive you. And if you pray now, one day you will be permitted to adore God for all eternity with the angels and the saints in Heaven.

In the Old Testament, we read that Jacob had a dream in which he saw a ladder reaching from the earth to Heaven, and angels were going up and down the ladder.[7] Prayer is like a ladder that reaches from earth to Heaven, and the angels constantly ascend and descend by it — that is, the angels carry your prayers to God's throne and bring God's grace to you.

Prayer is the bridge that spans the infinite abyss between Heaven and earth, between time and eternity. It is the golden bridge upon which God descends to you. St. Augustine called prayer "the key to Heaven" because it not only opens to us the treasures of divine grace, but also makes possible, by means of this grace, our entrance into Heaven. St. Teresa[8] said, "Promise me a quarter of an hour's prayer every day, and I, in the name of Jesus Christ, will promise you Heaven."

Your thoughts and desires are the food of your spiritual life. If you feed only on what is earthly and visible, you will never reach beyond these passing things. Ease in prayer is a sign that you are the master of the earthly desires and the sensuality of your nature, for in prayer you raise your thoughts to God and are in touch with Him.

Apart from Holy Communion, there is no more intimate union with God than by prayer. If you think of God and long for Him, you will share in the greatness of God. Praying is the most exalted act that you can perform.

Without prayer, you dare not face life. If you are out of touch with God, our Lady, and the saints, you cannot do your work

---

[7] Gen. 28:12.
[8] Probably St. Teresa of Avila (1515-1582), Carmelite nun and mystic. — ED.

or carry your burdens or hope to reach eternal life. Like one deprived of air and water, you will smother, dry up, and perish miserably.

∞

Prayer is an attitude of the soul

Prayer is not necessarily a matter of words. It is, as inspired by the Holy Spirit, fundamentally an active attitude of the soul. It is an attitude of eager longing for grace. It is a humble and trustful unfolding of your real needs before God, a pleading with Him to satisfy those needs, and a disposition to welcome these gifts of God, but, above all, a readiness to abandon yourself to God's will in all things. True prayer means the sincere will to exchange the life according to nature for the life according to God, to live in a childlike spirit of dependence on a heavenly Father and Creator.

Prayer of this kind is a key to happiness. The true cause of your unhappiness is that your longings are not for God, but for things other than God. You do not "seek first the kingdom of God and His justice."[9] God is more eager to give than you are to receive that which will bring about your happiness in this world and in the next. Our Lord said, "Blessed are they who hunger and thirst for justice, for they shall be satisfied."[10]

There are two kinds of people in this world: those seeking worldly pleasures and those seeking God. The latter find their happiness in knowing, loving, and serving God in this world so that they may be with Him in Heaven. The world cannot

---

[9] Matt. 6:33.
[10] Matt. 5:6 (RSV).

give true, lasting, and satisfying happiness, because man was not made for this world. God made man to find true happiness in Him alone. He has given us the means of keeping in touch with Him: prayer. Thus, after years of intimate union with God in prayer, St. Augustine could write, "You have made us for Yourself, O Lord, and our hearts are restless until they rest in You."[11]

Consequently, two great lessons must be learned about prayer. First, learn simplicity in prayer. It is easy to pray if you have good will. No learning, fluency of speech, mental quickness, or fervor of feeling is necessary. Look at God and give Him what you have, and that is, most of all, your good will. This is prayer.

The second lesson is that you must harmonize conduct with prayer. Prayer is the central activity of the Christian's life, his supreme interest, his highest privilege. It should be the dominating principle that binds together all his scattered acts.

Your life must have one controlling aim: you cannot afford to be in conflict and at cross-purposes with yourself. You will find the secret of this unity of plan in prayer. You are well on your way to happiness and holiness once you have fitted the rest of life into those aims and aspirations which are yours when you lift up your mind and will to God in prayer.

[11] *Confessions*, Bk. 1, ch. 1.

Chapter Two

∞

Learn why prayer is necessary

Prayer is necessary because God has commanded us to pray. The first commandment of God binds man to religion and worship of God: "I am the Lord thy God. . . . thou shalt not have strange gods before me."[12] The first commandment obliges us to offer to God alone the supreme worship that is due to Him. Man must recognize and honor God as his Creator. Religion consists in giving God the recognition and honor He deserves.

Prayer to God is an act of the virtue of religion, that highest of all the moral virtues that leads us to do our duty to our Creator by showing Him our respect and our submission. Created by God and totally dependent upon Him at every instant, we must always be in a state of reverence toward Him. When we pray, our mind, our noblest faculty, recognizes Him as Creator and Lord and expresses our need of Him.

In his encyclical letter *On the Liturgy*, Pope Pius XII wrote, "Genuine and real piety, which [St. Thomas Aquinas[13]] calls

[12] Exod. 20:2-3.
[13] St. Thomas Aquinas (c. 1225-1274), Dominican philosopher and theologian.

'devotion,' and which is the principal act of the virtue of religion — that act which correctly relates and fitly directs men to God and by which they freely and spontaneously give themselves to the worship of God in its fullest sense — *piety of this authentic sort needs meditation on the supernatural realities and spiritual exercises*, if it is to be nurtured, stimulated, and sustained, and if it is to prompt us to lead a more perfect life. For the Christian religion, practiced as it should be, demands that the will especially be consecrated to God and exert its influence on all the other spiritual faculties. But every act of the will presupposes an act of the intelligence, and before one can express the desire and the intention of offering oneself in sacrifice to the eternal Godhead, a knowledge of the facts and truths which make religion a duty is altogether necessary. But further, since our hearts, disturbed as they are at times by the lower appetites, do not always respond to motives of love, it is also extremely helpful to let consideration and contemplation of the justice of God provoke us on occasion to salutary fear, and guide us thence to Christian humility, repentance and amendment."[14]

Other virtues are involved in prayer, especially the theological virtues of faith, hope, and charity. Through faith we know God and His merciful power to which we appeal. Charity governs our desires and, in so doing, brings order into our petitions. Hope gives us the confident expectation that these desires will be granted. The virtues of humility and penance then cooperate with the virtue of religion to deepen our sentiments of reverence toward God.

[14] *Mediator Dei* (November 20, 1947), 32.

God requires prayer not because of any need of His, for He has need of nothing, but because of His justice and holiness. He is our Lord, our Father, the Source of all our good. Hence, honor is due to Him, and He cannot deny Himself by allowing this honor to be given to another. To refuse to pray is a form of denying God.

God owes you nothing unless you pray, because He has promised everything to those who pray.

You were created by God to know, love, praise, adore, and serve Him, and, thus, by prayer you attain your aim and purpose for living as far as you can do so on earth. Even in Heaven there will be eternal prayer.

Our Lord often taught the necessity of prayer: "Ask, and it shall be given you; seek, and you shall find";[15] "Watch and pray, that you may not enter into temptation";[16] "Amen, amen, I say to you, if you ask the Father anything in my name, He will give it to you."[17] Our Lord tells us we should "pray always," and St. Paul says, "Pray without ceasing,"[18] in the sense that we should always be ready to pray at the proper times and that our prayer should constantly influence our other actions.

⁂

Prayer obtains grace

Prayer is necessary because it is the great unconditional means of obtaining grace.

---

[15] Matt. 7:7.
[16] Matt. 26:41 (RSV).
[17] John 16:23.
[18] 1 Thess. 5:17.

Just as every river has a source that supplies it with water, and every kind of fruit owes its development to the sap of the tree on which it grows, so, too, the water of divine grace flowing into your soul must spring from some fountainhead and be replenished from it. So, also, whatever fruit good works produce in you must derive nourishment and strength from some source or fountainhead.

God, the Creator of the natural and the supernatural order, is indeed the ultimate source of all grace in man. But He does not always impart the water of grace to your soul immediately and without any channel to guide its flow. He develops, sustains, and increases the life-giving sap of grace within you only with some action on the part of your soul.

Only at the foot of high mountain ranges does water spring up copiously; from there it is carried through rivers or channels into various places. A tree receives the nourishing sap that makes it grow and produce fruit by sending its roots deep into the soil in search of nourishment and extending countless leaves in order to suck in the air's moisture.

The soil of your soul receives, through a sevenfold channel, the water of grace from the fountainhead that was opened on the heights of Calvary for the welfare of all mankind. These seven channels are the sacraments. The tree of your soul, with its blossoms and fruits, must constantly strive to draw down upon itself and breathe in the heavenly atmosphere of God's grace. This earnest striving of the soul heavenward in order to breathe in divine grace is prayer. The sacraments and prayer, together with good works, are the divinely instituted means of grace. Sacramentals — that is, holy things or actions of which the Church makes use to obtain for us from God, through her intercession, spiritual and temporal favors — if used with faith and devotion, also bring grace to your soul.[19]

We all need this important means of grace called prayer. Without it, it is impossible to lead a Christian life and to die a happy death.

Without divine grace, there is no salvation; without prayer, no grace can be looked for in those who have reached the age of reason. Prayer, therefore, is as necessary as grace itself. St. Thomas Aquinas states, "Every man is bound to pray to procure the spiritual good which God alone can give." Without the grace of God, you can do nothing in the supernatural order. You cannot overcome temptation or gain spiritual merit for any good deed performed.

After the Last Supper, Jesus said, "Without me, you can do nothing."[20] But the grace that you need is given, in God's ordinary Providence, only if you pray for it. God has arranged it so, in order that you may be conscious of your nothingness and remain humbly dependent upon Him.

God knows all your wants even before you express them to Him, and He is ever ready to help you. But He has established prayer as the condition for obtaining His grace and favors. Unless you observe this condition, how can you expect His help?

∞

Prayer is necessary for salvation

Moreover, because Original Sin has darkened your mind and weakened your will, you cannot long resist temptation or

---

[19] Sacramentals are discussed further in Chapter 21.
[20] John 15:5.

stay out of grave sin without the help of God's grace, which is given in answer to your prayer. Prayer is, therefore, the remedy for your human weakness. When you pray, God gives you the strength to do that which you, of yourself, cannot do.

St. Augustine wrote, "God does not command impossible things; but, by commanding, He suggests to you to do what you can and to ask for what is beyond your strength; and He helps you, that you may be able." This is practical advice. Do what you can, and pray to God for what you cannot do. You are weak, but God is strong. Through prayer, He communicates His strength to you, and you are able to do all things, as St. Paul declared: "I can do all things in Him who strengthens me."[21]

God has ordained the sacraments and prayer, along with good works, as the means whereby we are to obtain His grace. Only by free cooperation with God's plan can we be worthy of eternal salvation. Prayer is the least God can demand from us. If we must pray for temporal things, how much more must we pray for those that are eternal. The choice lies between prayer and spiritual ruin. By means of prayer, you provide yourself with all that is necessary for a good life.

Prayer is like light and air — nourishment for the spiritual life. Without prayer, the spiritual life cannot exist. If you want to be saved, then, you must pray.

∞

Prayer helps you to obey God's commandments

God gives to all the grace to pray, for He sincerely wills the salvation of every soul and provides every man with sufficient

---

[21] Phil. 4:13 (RSV).

grace to save his soul. That God sincerely wills the salvation of all men is evident both from the Holy Scriptures and from the constant teaching of the Church. St. Paul says, "I desire, therefore, first of all, that supplications, prayers, intercessions, and thanksgivings be made for all men. For this is good and agreeable in the sight of God our Savior, who will have all men to be saved and to come to the knowledge of the truth."[22] The Scriptures bring out clearly the fact that Jesus Christ, the Son of God, died to save all men: "For the Son of Man came to save what was lost";[23] "Christ died for all, in order that they who are alive may live no longer for themselves, but for Him who died for them and rose again."[24]

Since prayer is a necessary means for salvation, it is evident that God must give to every man the grace actually to pray, as the key to his salvation. If he makes use of prayer, all other graces come to him. If, on the other hand, he neglects to pray, he closes the door of eternal life upon himself.

You must keep God's commandments if you are to be saved, but of yourself you have neither the power nor the grace to keep them. God commands nothing that is impossible; He gives you the grace itself that you need or, at least, the power of prayer through which you receive that grace.

By your own natural strength, you cannot overcome temptations; but with God's help you can, and prayer is the means of gaining God's help. You are weak only because you do not pray. The saints were victorious because they prayed.

[22] 1 Tim. 2:1, 3-4.
[23] Matt. 18:11.
[24] 2 Cor. 5:15.

Temptation is not merely something that must be borne; it is rather a God-given opportunity to strengthen your soul, to gain merit for Heaven. One of the most important lessons you can learn in your life is how to face the many great and small and varied temptations you meet with each day.

Do not be disturbed at the presence of temptations in your mind or in your surroundings, but endeavor calmly to think of something else, to seek some other occupation, and especially to allow a little prayer to pass through your mind. For if, after a temptation, you can say that you prayed during it, and if you usually resist temptation, you can be absolutely sure that you did not consent to sin.

You cannot be saved without the grace of perseverance, and prayer is the means by which you obtain this grace.

It is an extraordinary gift to die in God's sanctifying grace. This gift of final perseverance cannot be merited, but it can be obtained through humble prayer. Prayer is a necessary means for salvation. God does not ordinarily grant His actual graces — especially that special grace of final perseverance — to those who do not pray.

Because of human weakness, you are of yourself unable to observe God's law, overcome temptations, and persevere to the end in the grace of God. However, with the help of His grace, you can do these things and save your soul. You obtain this grace through prayer. In prayer, you will find the key to your salvation. St. Alphonsus[25] sums up this wisdom in these words: "The man who prays will be saved; the man who does not pray

---

[25] St. Alphonsus Liguori (1696-1787), moral theologian and founder of the Redemptorists.

will be lost. The saints are in Heaven because they made use of prayer; the damned are in Hell because they refused to pray."

Therefore, it is your duty to pray. As an earnest Christian, you must pray much. St. John Chrysostom[26] wrote, "If you cease to pray, you act as if you were taking a fish out of the water, for as water is the life of the fish, likewise prayer must be the life of the Christian."

Our Christian religion began with prayer in the Cenacle[27] in Jerusalem. The pagans were astonished at the constant prayers of Christians, whose churches were true houses of prayer. Prayer is one of the great acts of religion, which is man's highest and most glorious possession in this world.

∞

Prayer is the basis of hope

The certitude of our Christian hope rests ultimately upon prayer. Hope is the virtue by which we firmly trust that God, who is all-powerful and faithful to His promises, will in His mercy give us eternal happiness and the means to obtain it. It is imposed upon every Christian as a command: "You that fear the Lord, hope in Him";[28] "Hope in thy God always."[29] St. Peter writes, "Set your hope fully upon that grace that is coming to you."[30]

[26] St. John Chrysostom (c. 347-407), Bishop of Constantinople.

[27] The Cenacle is the upper room in which the Last Supper took place and in which the Apostles prayed in preparation for the coming of the Holy Spirit.

[28] Ecclus. 2:9.

[29] Osee 12:6 (RSV = Hos. 12:6).

[30] 1 Pet. 1:13 (RSV).

This hope of eternal life ought to be sure and firm, as the Council of Trent expressly declared: "All men ought to place and repose a most firm hope in the help of God. For God, unless they fail to correspond to His grace, as He has begun the good work, so will He finish it, working in them both to will and to perform."[31]

The Christian virtue of hope rests certainly on the promise of God. God can and will save you, and has promised you all the necessary graces to enable you to obey His law, if you ask for them. Although hope is accompanied by fear, this fear is not imposed by God, but arises from yourself. It is possible for you at any time to fail by not corresponding with grace as you ought and by putting an obstacle in the way of grace by your sins. Therefore, do not trust in your own strength, but trust completely in the strength of God, certain of His good will and of His help, which will save you, provided that you pray for it.

The motives upon which the certainty of your hope is founded are the power and goodness of God, and His fidelity to His promises. Of these the strongest and most certain motive is God's infallible faithfulness to the promise that He has made to us, to save us through the merits of Jesus Christ and to give us the graces necessary for our salvation, if we pray for them. Our Lord made His promises in various ways: "Ask and you shall receive",[32] "If you ask the Father anything in my name, He will give it to you";[33] "He will give good things to

---

[31] Session 6, canon 13.
[32] John 16:24.
[33] John 16:23.

those that ask";[34] "I say to you, all things whatsoever you ask when you pray, believe that you shall receive them, and they shall come unto you."[35]

God has, then, bound Himself by His unfailing promises to answer every prayer that is made in the proper way. Upon this unshakable rock of God's fidelity, the certainty of our hope is founded. He gives to each of us the grace to pray.

If you pray, you will surely receive from God all the graces you need to overcome temptation, to avoid sin, and to attain eternal life. You need only fear that you will neglect to use the grace of prayer that God has given you. Pray much and well so that you may never neglect to use this great key to salvation.

∞

Prayer obtains favors from God

Prayer is necessary as a means to obtain favors from God. In prayer you humbly acknowledge your need and helplessness, and you give recognition to God's power, goodness, and faithfulness to His promises. When you pray, you worship God in your heart; you sanctify yourself, draw down upon yourself God's benefits, and prepare yourself to receive His grace.

We should pray with a conviction of our own helplessness and our dependence upon God. God is always ready to give us what we need, and by prayer we do not dispose Him to give, but prepare ourselves to receive. A teacher cannot give his knowledge to a child unless the child is willing to learn. So, unless we subject our will to God, we cannot gain union with

[34] Cf. Matt. 7:11.
[35] Cf. Mark 11:24.

God, nor can He give us what we need when we are not recep-
tive. Prayer puts us in the proper attitude of subjection of will
to God or readiness to receive gifts.

∞

Providence does not rule out prayer

Objections to prayer often arise from two opposite errors:
chance and fate. Chance means that all that happens takes
place without any kind of power to regulate it. Fate means that
everything is governed by rigid laws that cannot be controlled.
If the world turns on chance or fate, it is useless to pray.

But reason and revelation alike tell us that the world is
ruled by the Providence of God. We all firmly agree that there
is a law in the universe — the laws of nature — but at the
same time we believe that God, the Author of this law, can
counteract, suspend, or change it at His pleasure. Thus we
pray for health, fine weather, or rain, because we believe that
God is the Lord of Heaven and earth.

There may be times during the difficulties of life when we
forget that God is the Master of nature. We should remember
even during good times that we need the support of God's fatherly hand. Prayer will help us to remember that He is the
Maker and the Master of the universe and of all creatures.

∞

Prayer is necessary even though
God knows what you need

Another objection to prayer is that there is no need to pray
because God knows all things, and He is aware of all that is
necessary and useful to us.

We pray to God, not because He does not know our needs, but because it is His expressed wish that we ourselves should put them before Him. Although our Lord said, "Your Father knows that you need all these things,"[36] He also told us that we "must pray always and not lose heart."[37] The Our Father, that great prayer that our Lord Himself composed for us, contains a number of petitions.

While it is true that God knows all our needs even before we pray, this does not make prayer unnecessary. St. Thomas Aquinas wrote, "It is not necessary for us to set forth our petitions before God in order to make known to Him our needs or desires, but rather that we ourselves may realize that in these things it is needful to have recourse to the divine assistance."[38]

God does grant us many favors unasked, but there are many that He will grant only at our request. He wants us to ask for favors in order that through prayer we may be made aware of our utter dependence on Him for all things and in order that we may be reminded of His goodness to us. Pope St. Gregory I wrote, "Men, by petitioning, may merit to receive what Almighty God arranged before the ages to give them."[39]

Furthermore, when we pray, we cherish the hope of being heard, and we are less liable to forget God. As it is, mankind forgets Him all too often. Let us remember our Lord's command to "pray always" and go to Him not only in hours of distress, but in all events of this day called life.

---

[36] Matt. 6:32.
[37] Cf. Luke 18:1 (RSV).
[38] *Summa Theologica*, II-II, Q. 83, art. 2.
[39] Ibid.; St. Gregory the Great (c. 540-604), Pope from 590.

Chapter Three

Imitate the divine Model of prayer

As adopted children of God, we are obliged to strive to live a divine life. The eternal Son of God, the Divine Word and living Image of the Father, became man and showed us by His example how we could draw close to God. His Father pointed to Him as a model at His baptism and transfiguration when He said, "This is my beloved Son, in whom I am well pleased."[40] The eternal Father wants us to imitate His Son. Jesus Himself said, "I am the way, and the truth, and the life."[41]

God has willed that the salvation of mankind be accomplished not only by toil and suffering but also by prayer. That is why prayer played an important part in the life of Jesus.

∞

Jesus exemplified prayer amid ordinary tasks

Jesus entered life praying: "Behold, I come to do Thy will, O God."[42] During His infancy and childhood, when He was as

[40] Matt. 3:17, 17:5.
[41] John 14:6.
[42] Heb. 10:9.

yet unable to do other work, He was occupied in prayer. For thirty years, Jesus lived an ordinary, hidden, and prayerful life. Subject to Mary and Joseph, He labored as a carpenter. Thus He is the perfect Model for the great mass of men and women who have only ordinary duties to perform and who must work out their sanctification in humble occupations.

∞

Jesus exemplified different forms of prayer

What a perfect example of prayer our Savior set for us in His public life! Forty days of prayer and penance were the prelude to His short life as a missionary. He not only spoke often of prayer and encouraged and taught people to pray, but also practiced prayer Himself. Interiorly He enjoyed the constant vision of God, and therefore He was always engaged in inward communion with His Father.

• *Jesus prayed outwardly.* In His brief teaching career, He always found time for prayer, even prolonged prayer. He would rise very early to pray before He began His teaching, and He would leave the company of men in the evening to seek that of His Father in prayer. "He went out to the mountain to pray, and continued all night in prayer to God."[43]

• *Jesus prayed publicly and vocally.* One day, the disciples found Him praying. When He finished, one of them said to Him, "Lord, teach us to pray, as John also taught his disciples." And Jesus said, "When you pray, say, 'Our

---

[43] Luke 6:12.

Father . . .' "[44] Then He taught them the most beautiful prayer ever composed.

After the Our Father, the most sublime prayer of Jesus was the high-priestly prayer He uttered at the Last Supper. Raising His eyes to Heaven, He said, "Father, the hour has come! Glorify Thy Son, that Thy Son may glorify Thee, as Thou hast given Him power over all flesh, that He may give eternal life to all whom Thou hast given Him. Now, this is everlasting life: that they may know Thee, the only true God, and Jesus Christ, whom Thou hast sent."[45]

In his encyclical letter *On the Mystical Body of Christ*, Pope Pius XII wrote, "Our Redeemer showed His burning love for the Church especially by praying for her to His heavenly Father. To recall but a few examples . . . just before the crucifixion He prayed repeatedly for Peter,[46] for the other Apostles,[47] for all who, through the preaching of the holy Gospel, would believe in Him.[48]

"After the example of Christ, we too should pray daily to the Lord of the harvest to send laborers into His harvest.[49] Our united prayer should rise daily to Heaven for all the members of the Mystical Body of Jesus Christ. Likewise, we must earnestly desire that this united

[44] Cf. Luke 11:1-2.
[45] John 17:1-3.
[46] Luke 22:32.
[47] John 17:9-19.
[48] John 17:20-23.
[49] Matt. 9:38.

prayer may embrace in the same ardent charity both those who, not yet enlightened by the truth of the Gospel, are still without the fold of the Church, and those who, on account of regrettable schism, are separated from us, who though unworthy, represent the person of Jesus Christ on earth."[50]

• *Jesus prayed at ordinary times* in the synagogue and elsewhere on various occasions. Before the crowds, He said, "I thank Thee, Father, Lord of Heaven and earth, that Thou hast hidden these things from the wise and understanding and revealed them to babes. Yea, Father, for such was Thy gracious will."[51]

• *Jesus prayed before undertaking any important projects.* Before He chose His twelve Apostles, He prayed all night.[52] Before the great miracle of the multiplication of the loaves, He prayed in thanksgiving.[53] Before raising Lazarus to life, Jesus lifted His eyes and said, "Father, I give Thee thanks that Thou hast heard me. And I knew Thou hearest me always; but because of the people who stand about I have said it, that they may believe that Thou hast sent me."[54]

• *Jesus closed His life with prayer.* He asked not for justice, but for mercy and pardon for those who were putting

[50] *Mystici Corporis Christi* (June 29, 1943), 100-102.
[51] Matt. 11:25-26 (RSV).
[52] Luke 6:12.
[53] John 6:11.
[54] John 11:41-42.

Him to death: "Father, forgive them, for they know not
what they do."[55] When His own Father seemed to have
abandoned Him, He sought relief for His dejected soul
in the heart-piercing cry: "My God, my God, why hast
Thou forsaken me?"[56] After giving forgiveness to unre-
pentant enemies, His kingdom to the penitent thief,
His Mother to John and John to His Mother, and His
Blood to the earth, He kept His soul for His Father. He
yielded it up to God as He cried out with a loud voice,
"Father, into Thy hands I commend my spirit."[57] The
supreme act of His life was completely achieved by a
prayer of trustful love to His heavenly Father.

∽

*The glorified life of Jesus is
entirely absorbed by prayer*

In the Holy Eucharist, Jesus is always in loving adoration
before His heavenly Father, taking delight in contemplating
the infinite perfections of the triune God and honoring Him
by His prayer-life in the tabernacle. He never interrupts His
prayer for a single moment. This homage, rising from altars
the whole world over, is of infinite value, because it is offered
by the very Son of God Himself.

In the Eucharist, Jesus also occupies Himself with the interests of mankind. He thanks God for us, prays continually
for us, asks pardon for our sins, and makes constant reparation

[55] Luke 23:34.
[56] Matt. 27:46.
[57] Luke 23:46.

and amends for them. He is always offering Himself in sacrifice to God and pouring out His graces upon all mankind as our Eucharistic Mediator.

In Heaven, Jesus is the Representative and High Priest of all humanity. He honors His Father and implores heavenly help for us. As St. Paul says, "He is able at all times to save those who draw near to God through Him, since He lives always to make intercession for them."[58] By His prayer of mediation, as also by His doctrine, His labors, and His sufferings, He sustains the whole Church and every individual.

In his encyclical letter *On Devotion to the Sacred Heart*, Pope Pius XII wrote, "As Christ loved the Church with that triple love of which we have spoken, He still loves her most deeply. This love moves Him as our Advocate to gain grace and mercy for us from the Father, 'since He lives always to make intercession for them.' The prayers that come forth from His inexhaustible love and are directed to the Father are never interrupted. As 'in the days of His earthly life,'[59] so, now triumphant in Heaven, He beseeches the Father with no less efficacy. . . .

"It is then absolutely certain that the heavenly Father 'who has not spared even His own Son, but has delivered Him for us all'[60] when He has been asked by so powerful an Advocate and with such ardent love, will never at any time diminish the rich flow of divine graces to all men."[61]

---

[58] Heb. 7:25 (RSV).
[59] Heb. 5:7.
[60] Rom. 8:32.
[61] *Haurietis aquas* (May 15, 1956), 105, 107.

∽

Jesus prays in the Mass

The prayer of Jesus in the Garden of Gethsemane was an expression of the prayer of His life — namely, His unchanging submission to the will of God.[62] "My food is to do the will of Him who sent me."[63] At the beginning, His attitude is declared in the words: "Behold, I come to do Thy will, O God." At the end of life, He could say, "I have accomplished the work that Thou hast given me to do."[64]

Even now, after He has ascended into Heaven, Jesus Christ renews, throughout time, the perfect offering of Himself to the Father by the Sacrifice of the Mass. Each Mass shows forth His death, which was a sacrifice in blood upon the Cross. In each Mass, the same High Priest offers Himself, by the hands of His priests, in an unbloody manner, perpetuating the Sacrifice of the Cross and applying to us the fruits of His Redemption.

The soul of that sacrifice is the interior offering of Christ, which was once made manifest by the shedding of His Blood and by His words upon the Cross: "It is consummated";[65] "Father, into Thy hands I commend my spirit."

That offering of infinite value continues to exist in the heart of Jesus Christ and, as adoration and thanksgiving, will continue forever. Since the price paid is infinite, there is no grace for which you may not hope, begging it through the divine Mediator.

[62] "Not my will, but Thine be done" (Luke 22:42).
[63] John 4:34 (RSV).
[64] John 17:4.
[65] John 19:30.

ॐ

Christ prayed for your sake

Why was Jesus so constant in prayer? First, it was fitting and necessary that He do so as our exemplar.

Also, since He was a creature insofar as His human nature was concerned, He was bound to offer to the Father the tribute of prayer, adoration, and thanksgiving. Jesus regarded prayer as something most sublime, because it is conversation with God. Nothing was higher, sweeter, or more important to Him.

Jesus also prayed in order to make our prayer effective by means of His own prayer, to gain graces for us, and to glorify God in us. He did not need to pray for graces for Himself but for us. As a member of the human race, He was subject to the same law that governs us: the more prayer, the more grace; the less prayer, the less grace; no prayer, no grace. God required of Him not only work and suffering, but also prayer as the price of the grace that mankind was to receive through His merits.

Jesus had all humanity to pray for and much to ask for in its behalf. He regarded Himself as — and He really was — the Representative, the Head, and the High Priest of the whole human race. He was the Mediator between God and man. St. Paul says, "In the days of His flesh, Jesus offered up prayers and supplications, with loud cries and tears, to Him who was able to save Him from death, and He was heard for His reverence."[66]

Thus, Jesus had before His mind each individual human being, with his wants, concerns, duties, dangers, and difficulties. He saw in spirit the whole Church as well as the entire

---

[66] Cf. Heb. 5:7 (RSV).

human race, both of which draw their life from His intercession, His grace, and His doctrine. His were truly the prayers of
the God-Man.

∝

Jesus desires union with you

At the Last Supper, our Lord expressed His last will to His
disciples in these words: "Abide in me, and I in you."[67] He
wished that they remain united to Him in spirit. This union
was to be so close and vital that Jesus used the beautiful example of the vine and the branches to symbolize it.[68] As the
branch is united to the vine and has a common life with it, so
are men to be united with Him. Christ is the spiritual Vine
that supports and gives life to the whole Church and to the entire human race.

At the Last Supper, Jesus made it clear that this vital union
is to be maintained through the Holy Eucharist, which He had
just established, and also through prayer. This prayer, He
taught, is to be made in His name. "Whatever you shall ask in
my name, that I will do, that the Father may be glorified in the
Son. If you shall ask me anything in my name, that I will do."[69]
To pray in the name of Jesus means that we unite ourselves to
Him by faith and love; that we pray for His intentions, which
are the advancement and welfare of the kingdom of God; that
we rely upon His merits; that we invoke His Father in His
name; and that we pray at His desire.

[67] John 15:4.
[68] Cf. John 15:1-5.
[69] John 14:13-14.

At the Last Supper, Jesus gave us the most beautiful motives for prayer.

• *He spoke of prayer as a proof of faith and the glorification of God.* "Whatever you ask in my name, that I will do, in order that the Father may be glorified in the Son." Prayer is a very important part of apostolic work. "You have not chosen me, but I have chosen you and have appointed you that you should go and bear fruit, and that your fruit should remain; that whatever you ask the Father in my name He may give you."[70] Prayer is the mightiest means of promoting Christ's kingdom, because it is always at our command and its effects can extend over all places and times.

• *Jesus spoke of prayer as a means of union with Him.* Through prayer, we are to receive and absorb the life-giving sap of the Vine. "If you abide in me, and my words abide in you, you shall ask whatever you will and it shall be done unto you. In this is my Father glorified, that you may bring forth very much fruit, and become my disciples."[71] Through prayer, we grow in faith and love.

• *Jesus spoke of prayer as a substitute for His bodily presence.* What our Savior did for the Apostles as long as He was visibly with them He will now do by means of prayer. Prayer was to teach them, protect and comfort them, and provide them with all they needed. He said,

[70] John 15:16.
[71] John 15:7-8.

"Hitherto you have not asked anything in my name. Ask, and you shall receive, that your joy may be full."[72] By faith in Him and love for Him, by compliance with His intentions and by union with His merits, the prayer of the Apostles would become, as it were, His own prayer and would, therefore, be all-powerful. He said, "If you ask me anything in my name, I will do it"; "If you ask the Father anything in my name, He will give it to you."[73]

A prayer in the name of Jesus does not even need any special recommendation or help from Him, for He said, "In that day, you shall ask in my name; and I say not to you that I will ask the Father for you, for the Father Himself loveth you, because you have loved me, and have believed that I came forth from God."[74] What motives more beautiful and more sublime than these could urge you to pray!

༈

The Our Father is the perfect prayer
When the apostles asked Jesus to teach them to pray, He gave them and us the perfect prayer. He said, "In this manner, therefore, shall you pray: 'Our Father who art in Heaven . . .' "[75] The Our Father is a prayer of perfect and unselfish love, because, in saying it, we offer ourselves entirely to God and ask

---

[72] John 16:24.
[73] John 16:23.
[74] John 16:26-27.
[75] Matt. 6:9.

Him for the best things, not only for ourselves but also for our neighbor.

It is quite important for you to fill your prayers with the spirit of the Lord's Prayer:

"Our Father, who art in Heaven."
O God, You are our last end.
To possess You on earth and someday
in Heaven is my only true happiness.
That I may possess You,
give me childlike trust and love.

"Hallowed by Thy name."
As Your loving child, I am eager for
Your interests, O heavenly Father.
Let Your honor be my primary concern.

"Thy kingdom come."
Since love seeks intimate union,
I desire not only that You should rule
more and more human hearts,
but also that You should reign ever more fully
over my will and the wills of all men.

"Thy will be done on earth as it is in Heaven."
My heavenly Father, I believe that I
can reach eternal happiness by fulfilling
Your holy will daily. I ask You to aid me to do
Your holy will in all things, as Your will is
accomplished by the angels and saints in Heaven.
And this life in Heaven is a model of perfect
union between Creator and creature.

"Give us this day our daily bread."
By living my human life as I ought,
may I conform myself to Your will.
For a complete life, I need good things
for soul and body. I look to You
to supply me with both.

"Forgive us our trespasses
as we forgive those who trespass against us,
and lead us not into temptation."
Sin throws itself between my soul and You,
O God. Strengthen me in temptation,
because it is a constant danger to
the friendship between me, Your creature,
and You, my Creator.

"But deliver us from evil."
O God, I beg You not to permit me
to give up and prove faithless under the
heavy crosses of life. Preserve me from
the greatest of all evils: mortal sin.

When you pray the Our Father, do you use the age-old words to mean what our Lord meant them to mean, or does your prayer go something like this? "Our Father, who art in Heaven, ready to lend me a hand whenever I call for it, listen! This is what I want. I want my own little kingdom here, with everyone kowtowing to me; I want my name to be honored by everyone; I want my will to be done by Thee and by everyone else. Give me not only bread, but pie and ice cream and a fat checking account, so that I won't have to ask You for what I need each day. Oh, yes, and forgive all my sins, even though there are persons whom I can't forgive, because they are just too hateful to be let off easily. But forgive me anyway, because I don't want to go to Hell or Purgatory or have anything bad happen to me. Lead me not into temptation, but don't be angry if I get there on my own. And deliver me from bad luck. Amen."

This Our Father is not a prayer of perfect and unselfish love, because, in saying it, you do not offer yourself entirely to God, nor do you ask from Him the best things for yourself and your neighbor. How often we are inclined to mix a little of the wrong Our Father into the right one.

∞

Prayer is a great and necessary duty

Following the example of Jesus, you, too, must pray, because there is nothing higher and nothing better than to converse with God — and nothing more necessary. Strive for union with Jesus through prayer, because this will ensure your own progress in virtue. Jesus is your way, your truth, and your life. He is the only way that leads to the Father; there is no other. In Him, you must grow until you attain your full stature in Heaven. By means of this union with Jesus in prayer, you will be one with Him in truth, in strength, and in merits; He will be praying in you! What glorious strength and power this union with Christ gives you to glorify God and save the world!

Pray as Jesus did; that is, pray much — as much as the duties of your vocation demand and permit. You will learn to pray well by praying as our Savior prayed, with the desire that God may be gloried in you and in others. You will pray well when you pray not only for yourself and for your own little domestic wants and needs, but for the whole Church and for the entire human race. Thus you will be praying much and long — for you will have to pray for many and ask for much.

In the prayer-life of Jesus, everyone can find a lesson and a model. Seeking God as one's last end is the highest duty of man. Nothing is more important for you than to be in close union with God, for it is within this union that sanctity is essentially achieved. Prayer was dear to the heart of Christ because through prayer alone is union with God attained. Pray because He recommends that you pray and because He also prays. Remember that His example is equivalent to a command. Pray because your prayer is for you the means of salvation and perfection.

Chapter Four

☙

Recognize the power of prayer

As prayer is a necessary means of obtaining every need, so it is also sufficient for everything.

The power of prayer comes from the promise that Jesus made concerning prayer, as He so beautifully shows: "Ask, and it shall be given you; seek, and you shall find; knock, and it shall be opened to you. For everyone who asks receives; and he who seeks finds; and to him who knocks, it shall be opened."[76] His promise is a solemn one by which He pledges His divine word. It is a comprehensive and unconditional promise, limited only by our welfare and the glory of God. Miracles are not excluded. Prayer has worked many. Even Heaven is included; indeed, Heaven especially, and before all else. "If you ask the Father anything in my name, He will give it to you. . . . Ask, and you shall receive, that your joy may be full."[77]

Prayer, then, is infallible — that is, it will always be heard, not because of any power on our part, but because of Christ's promise that He will not fail to answer our prayers. Even the

[76] Matt. 7:7-8 (RSV).
[77] John 16:23-24.

prayers of those in mortal sin are infallibly heard, if they sincerely want to repent, as did the thief on the cross.

∞

The power of prayer depends on
God's infinite goodness and mercy

The reason your petitions are granted is not your worthiness and merit, but the infinite mercy of God. If your merit were the reason, you would not petition, but demand; but as it is, you ask. And so you must have faith and trust in God's goodness and mercy.

The power of God's answer extends as far as your need and His divine mercy. You may pray for whatever you desire, whatever is reasonable and pleasing to God — especially spiritual gifts. The more necessary and the more excellent the gift, the more confidently you may trust that it will be granted to you. If you pray for temporal gifts and it seems as though God has not heard you, remember that the only reason He does not grant them is that He knows they would prove harmful to you. If temporal gifts are denied, you can be sure that God has some greater gift to bestow.

Holy Scripture has splendid pictures of the power of prayer: Israel in the desert, Moses and Joshua, the mighty deeds of the judges and the Maccabees, the miracles of our Lord and the Apostles, and the whole history of God's chosen people and of the early Catholic Church. Prayer figures in a constant and marvelous exchange between human need and divine help.

Jesus told the people several parables in which He stressed the goodness and mercy of God in answering prayer. He spoke of a judge who, although unjust, was willing to help a poor widow because she appealed to him with all the fervor of her heart.[78] How much more will the just God hear us, His own children!

Jesus spoke of a man who went to his neighbor at night to beg for some bread for a friend who had just arrived from a long journey. Because he continued to knock, his neighbor was compelled to get up and grant his request even in the middle of the night.[79] Such is the effect of perseverance in prayer.

Our Lord also mentioned the willingness of a father to come to the aid of his child when that child begs for help. The father will not offer the child a snake or a stone when he asks for food. If we, imperfect as we are, do these things for our children, then certainly the heavenly Father, who is goodness itself, will give us good things when we ask Him.[80]

And if mothers are so sensitive to the needs of their children, how much more the Father and Creator of all mankind must be alert to the needs of His children when they speak to Him in prayer! A mother's love is a spark compared with the burning furnace of God's infinite love for us, His creatures. If mothers are so ready to help when they hear their children in need, how can God our Father fail to hear your voice when you cry to Him in prayer?

And all the tender affection He pours out upon countless other souls does not lessen His love for you. His care of the entire universe is insignificant compared with the care He has for your immortal soul.

[78] Luke 18:2-8.
[79] Luke 11:5-8.
[80] Luke 11:11-13.

∞

The state of grace gives power to your soul

Consider the power of the prayer of a soul in the state of grace. By the fact that you are in the state of grace, your prayer has a power over the heart of God that, in a certain sense, is absolute.

Your prayer is the cry of a child to God his Father. For God, in seeing you as redeemed by the Precious Blood of His beloved Son, beholds no longer a mere human creature. He sees instead the reflection of His own divine life, for when you are in the state of grace, your entire being shares in the life of the triune God. Your prayer, then, partakes of that which is properly divine. By grace, you are a member of the family of God, our Father, and you have been given a right to the eternal inheritance of the Beatific Vision.

If you are in the state of grace, your prayer has another claim on God: it is always made in the name of Jesus Christ. You will not, in your own sinfulness, presume to ask, but you speak in the name of Jesus, by His own command. Our Lord Himself assures you, "Whatsoever you ask in my name, that I will do, that the Father may be glorified in the Son."[81]

When you are in the state of grace, your prayer is assisted by God the Holy Spirit. "The Promise of the Father"[82] dwells in your heart. "The Spirit helps us in our weakness, for we do not know how to pray as we ought, but the Spirit Himself intercedes for us with unutterable groanings."[83] The Holy

---

[81] John 14:13.
[82] Luke 24:49.
[83] Cf. Rom. 8:26 (RSV).

Spirit teaches you how to pray, because He inspires you to ask for what is right. He arouses in you desires that, under His influence, can be helpful to your salvation.

However, for prayer to be meritorious, you must be in the state of grace. Prayer makes satisfaction to God for your sins; it increases sanctifying grace in your soul as well as the virtues and gifts of the Holy Spirit. Prayer secures from God the help you need, both spiritual and temporal, to live a good and happy life and to save your soul, not by influencing God or by changing His unalterable will, but by fitting yourself to receive the gifts that He has determined from all eternity to grant to you through your prayers.

∞

Prayer is a powerful force that is at your disposal

Jesus taught that through prayer you can ask for every gift, whether it be for the gifts of the Holy Spirit or for the daily bread you need. You can use prayer to storm Heaven and secure its treasures and thus reach the heart of God. Through prayer you can win untold graces and blessings and favors for yourself and for the whole human race.

Prayer wins for yourself and others the things that make life happy and eternity sure. Do not neglect to pray for others. St. John Chrysostom wrote, "We are compelled to pray for ourselves, but the love of our brethren engages us to pray for others also. Now, far more acceptable to God is the prayer that proceeds not from the pressure of our wants, but from the love of our neighbor."

Use this powerful gift of prayer to win blessings for the world that does not pray, forgiveness for sinners who do not ask for forgiveness, and faith for those who have never heard the name of Christ or who have heard it only to turn away toward worldly pursuits. You can obtain strength and God's willing assistance for all mankind. Pope St. Gregory writes, "He causes his prayers to be of more avail to himself who offers them also for others."

You can never be grateful enough to the merciful God, who has given you this power. You can do no less than use this power as readily as He would have you use it. God does His part. He has given you the power of prayer and is willing to hear your prayer. He is able to grant your requests. The only thing that remains for you to do is to use this power of prayer as Christ meant you to use it. Prayer is the key that opens the treasury of God. You have the key. Use it well and often!

Part Two

∽

Practice the forms
of prayer

Chapter Five

Practice vocal prayer

There are two broad divisions of prayer: vocal and mental. We shall consider these forms of prayer in some detail so that our notion of prayer may be well rounded and as accurate as possible.

Vocal prayer is prayer in word or action. Since man is composed of soul and body, he must use not only his mind in prayer, but also his body and its senses for the glory of God. You express your interior sentiments and reverence for God in articulated words or in bodily posture, such as kneeling, standing, bowing, or folding your hands. Vocal prayer can be as pleasing to God and as useful to you as mental prayer is.

In this kind of prayer, the words you use when conversing with God are only a vehicle. They are less important than the love conveyed through them, for prayer is a lifting up of mind and will to God. Since the words are so much less important than love, it really makes little difference whether they are well chosen and nicely arranged. The great value of a vocal prayer always lies in the fact that it is a means by which you lovingly adore God. Each prayer is useful to the degree that it lifts the mind and will to God.

Of course, certain prayers do have the power to awaken fervor and move the will. Such prayers are acts of faith, hope, and charity, the Our Father, and the Hail Mary.

In vocal prayer, we use a prepared form of words, either a standard prayer from a prayer book or a prayer we have made up ourselves, and we recite this prayer, aloud or silently, from the book or from memory. In mental prayer, we do not use a prepared form of words at all, but merely raise our minds and hearts to God spontaneously, addressing Him with words of love, or in no words at all. Of course, a genuine interior devotion must be present in both vocal and mental prayer. Your morning and evening prayer, your meal prayers, the Rosary, and litanies are private vocal prayers.

∞

Invoking the saints aids vocal prayer

The practice of invoking the saints keeps before your mind the consoling doctrine of the Communion of Saints and of the universal motherhood of Mary. We help one another here on earth by mutual prayer; we pray, too, for our beloved dead and for all the souls in Purgatory; and to the saints in glory we look for assistance, calling on them to intercede for us with God. In this way, we can keep alive the family spirit that binds together the brothers and sisters of Jesus Christ, under the fatherhood of God and the motherhood of our Blessed Lady.

Devotion to our Lady is a sort of echo of our Lord's bidding to become like little children if we wish to enter the kingdom of Heaven.[84] Our Blessed Mother enters largely — as in a

---

[84] Cf. Matt. 18:3.

lesser degree the other saints also enter — into the scheme of salvation.

∞

Vocal prayer forms an essential part
of the external worship of God

The Church follows the example of our Savior, who prayed orally and taught His disciples to pray in the same way. She attaches great importance to prayer that is offered by the faithful in groups, such as at public services in churches, at Mass, during novenas, and at Benediction.

Public prayer has a special power with God and is very pleasing to Him, for our Lord said, "If two of you agree on earth about anything they ask, it will be done for them by my Father in Heaven. For where two or three are gathered in my name, there am I in the midst of them."[85] Jesus is near them with His grace and will support their prayers by His intercession with the Father.

∞

The Liturgy is the corporate prayer of the Church

The Liturgy of the Church is made up of the prayers said during the Holy Sacrifice of the Mass, the Divine Office, and the prayers used in the administration of the sacraments and sacramentals. The Liturgy never represents the prayer of a single individual, praying in his own name for his own purposes, but rather the prayer of the whole Church, praying to God as one body, the Mystical Body of Christ.

[85] Matt. 18:19-20 (RSV).

In his encyclical letter *On the Liturgy*, Pope Pius XII wrote, "The Divine Redeemer has so willed it that the priestly life, begun with the supplication and sacrifices of His mortal body, should continue without intermission down the ages in His Mystical Body, which is the Church.

"In obedience . . . to her Founder's behest, the Church *prolongs the priestly mission of Jesus Christ mainly by means of the sacred Liturgy.* She does this in the first place at the altar, where constantly the Sacrifice of the Cross is re-presented and, with a single difference in the manner of its offering, renewed. She does it next by means of the sacraments, whose special channels through which men are made partakers in the supernatural life. She does it finally by offering to God, all good and great, the daily tribute of her prayer of praise. 'What a spectacle for Heaven and earth,' observes Our Predecessor of happy memory, Pius XI, 'is not the Church at prayer! For centuries without interruption, from midnight to midnight, the divine psalmody of the inspired canticles is repeated on earth; there is no hour of the day that is not hallowed by its special Liturgy; there is no stage of human life that has not its part in the thanksgiving, praise, supplication, and reparation of this common prayer of the Mystical Body of Christ! . . .' "[86]

The Church is called the Mystical Body of Christ because her members — in Heaven, on earth, and in Purgatory — are united by supernatural bonds with one another and with Christ, their Head. Thus, all together they resemble the parts of the living human body. Christ is the Light of the World.[87]

[86] *Mediator Dei*, 2, 3.
[87] John 8:12.

The light of each individual is sanctifying grace, which, like a light in each soul, unites all the members of the Church.

The doctrine of the Communion of Saints — the union of the faithful on earth, the blessed in Heaven, and the souls in Purgatory, with Christ as their Head — assures you that you have millions of friends, bound to you by the supernatural bond of divine grace and charity flowing from Christ.

In his encyclical letter *On the Liturgy*, Pope Pius XII wrote, "Along with the Church . . . *her divine Founder is present at every liturgical function:* Christ is present at the August Sacrifice of the Altar both in the person of His minister and above all under the Eucharistic species. He is present in the sacraments, infusing into them the power which makes them ready instruments of sanctification. He is present finally in the prayer of praise and petition we direct to God, as it is written: 'Where there are two or three gathered together in my name, there am I in the midst of them.' *The sacred Liturgy is consequently the public worship which our Redeemer as Head of the Church renders to the Father as well as the worship which the community of the faithful renders to its Founder, and through Him to the Heavenly Father. It is,* in short, the worship rendered by the Mystical Body of Christ in the entirety of its Head and members."[88]

∞

*Liturgical prayer includes adoration,
praise, reparation, and petition*

Liturgical prayer is, first of all, an offering of adoration and praise. It is the joyful recognition of God's supreme majesty

---

[88] *Mediator Dei*, 20.

and His dominion over us and our complete submission and consecration to Him. This is the most excellent and the most precious service God can receive from us. Liturgical prayer is like an echo of that eternal hymn of praise that the blessed in Heaven are forever singing before the throne of God.

But reparation and petition also have their part in the Liturgy. Christ prays for us as our High Priest. He prays in us as our Head. That is why the eternal Father cannot separate us from Christ, any more than the head can be separated from the body. In seeing us, He sees His Son, for we are one with Him. The Father finds His glory in loving His Son. In granting us what His Son asks in us, He is "glorified in His Son."

Jesus promised, "Whatever you ask in my name, I will do it, that the Father may be glorified in the Son."[89] The Church uses the phrase "in the name of Jesus Christ our Lord" or its equivalent in all her important prayers. At Holy Mass, the great prayers end with the invocation "through Christ our Lord. Amen." This means that those who pray know that their prayers and petitions are backed by the power and approval of Jesus Christ. They ask, not by themselves alone, but in partnership with the Son of God, whom the heavenly Father cannot refuse. If you pray and call upon the name of Christ, you really enter into a form of partnership with Him.

When you take part in a liturgical ceremony, you are united to the whole Church in virtue of a real and active cooperation in an act of religion, which the Church as a society offers to God. Unite yourself to Jesus, joining your prayers to those He made here below, especially to that sublime prayer

[89] John 14:13 (RSV).

54

which, as Mediator and High Priest, He unceasingly continues in Heaven for you and all mankind. He is the way to the Father.

∝

The Mass is the center of public worship
The center and the soul of the public worship of the Church is the Holy Sacrifice of the Mass. At this most sacred function, the eternal High Priest Himself stands in the assembly of the faithful, in order to offer sacrifice for them and make intercession for them. At the altar, the three great provinces of the kingdom of God — the Church Militant, the Church Suffering, and the Church Triumphant — take part, according to the needs and powers of each, in the Blessings of the eucharistic sacrifice.

While at Mass, confidently pray to God through our Lord, who makes you rich with His own merits and whose prayer is always pleasing to God. He makes up for your misery and unworthiness. Unite yourself in spirit with the entire Mystical Body of Christ — the Holy Father, bishops, priests, religious — and with the Church Triumphant — the choirs of the angels and saints and your heavenly Mother — to offer God this homage of adoration, thanksgiving, reparation, and petition.

Try to learn as much as you can about the meaning of the Liturgy and to participate in it actively, for Pope St. Pius X[90] said, "The active participation of the laity in the liturgical prayer and life of the Church is the primary and indispensable source of the true Christian spirit."

[90] St. Pius X (1835-1914), Pope from 1903.

∞

Family prayer brings God into the home

Prayer and the sacraments are the ordinary sources of grace for the individual and for the family as well. Happiness reigns in the home insofar as these sources of grace are used, because they are the means of bringing God into the home. Parents who are deeply religious and are convinced that religion is not something just to be believed, but something to be lived, will encourage family prayers in the home.

Back in the third century, St. Cyprian[91] indicated that group or family prayers were in keeping with the spirit of the first Christians: "We do not say *my* Father, neither do we say give *me*, but give *us*; and this because the Teacher of unity did not wish prayer to be made privately, that is, that each should pray for himself alone; for He wished one to pray for all, since He in His single Person had borne all."

∞

Parents must be prayerful

Some parents seem to think that their responsibilities to their children are chiefly material in nature. Of far greater importance is the spiritual care of their children's souls. They are bound in conscience to give them a Catholic education, or at least provide for their religious education. They have the duty of helping their children choose a profession or vocation and of preparing them for it. Parents must guard their children against sin, aid them in the practice of virtue, counsel them in their problems, instruct them, and, above all, pray for them.

[91] St. Cyprian (c. 258), Bishop of Carthage.

In order that parents may fulfill their office worthily, they must be what God intends them to be. They cannot impart character, virtue, and nobility if they do not themselves have these qualities. Parents cannot teach respect for God, religion, and themselves if they do not show by their words and actions that they respect God, religion, and themselves. Parents cannot expect children to be faithful in their duties toward them if they are unfaithful in their duties toward their children. Without God and religion, parents cannot hope to meet and solve the problems and difficulties of married life. If children see that their parents love God and their neighbor and practice their religion conscientiously, they will be drawn to imitate their example.

All this demands that parents be prayerful, because through prayer they bring God into their family life and obtain His grace to carry out faithfully their duties toward each other and toward their children.

The family Rosary is a practical way to strengthen family unity, so easily weakened by the modern way of life. It protects family life from worldliness and worldly doctrines. It is a source of great blessing for the family, perhaps the greatest of which is peace founded on love.

Family prayer is most salutary in bringing life in the home to its full splendor by raising the family to a higher family circle where God is Father and Mary is Mother and all are children of God.

Chapter Six

ஃ

Practice mental prayer

Mental prayer, or meditation, is distinguished from vocal prayer because in its use one does not observe a set form of prayer or any arranged sequence of words, and because it consists in a serious consideration of the truths of Faith, with a view to their practical application to daily life. This consideration is but the preparation that is to lead to prayer, properly so called, and to more ardent and fervent communion with God. Prayer is always conversation with God.

In mental prayer, or meditation, you apply the three powers of your soul to prayer: your memory, your understanding, and your will. Your memory recalls a religious or moral truth, your understanding considers this truth and applies it to your personal life, and your will strongly makes practical resolutions and desires to translate this truth into action.

ஃ

Meditation is simple

Mental prayer is not too high and difficult for you. When you reflect on whether you should undertake some act and how you should accomplish it, this mental reflection is a serious consideration. A similar consideration, when applied to the spiritual life, and accompanied with prayers, constitutes a real meditation.

There are many ways to make a meditation. One of the simplest is to re-create in your imagination the lovable figure of Christ in one of the mysteries of His earthly life: to see Him in the crib or on the Cross; to listen to His voice; to imagine the surroundings, the people, and the circumstances; to make this picture as realistic as possible; and then to abandon your heart to the acts of love that the scene inspires.

The following is a simple plan of meditation suggested by St. Ignatius of Loyola:[92]

• Ask the Holy Spirit to help you in your meditation.

• Choose a subject to meditate on. For example, Jesus' death on the Cross.

• Ask yourself questions such as: Who? What? Where? Why? When? How? How many? How often? With what help? With what results? For example: *Who* is dying on the Cross? *Who* has profited by Christ's Passion? *What* does Jesus suffer? *What* can I do to console Jesus?

• Give an answer to each question. For example: Jesus, my Savior and my God, is dying on the Cross.

• Talk to God about the things suggested by your answers. For example: Jesus, forgive me for having caused Your sufferings. Thank You for having saved my soul.

---

[92] St. Ignatius of Loyola (1495-1556), founder of the Jesuits.

Remember: prayer is conversation with God. Each answer will suggest something to speak about. Continue on that topic of conversation as long as you can, and do not worry about being particular about logical order. The important thing is to keep up your conversation with God. Sometimes you will lift your soul to God in thanksgiving and adoration and love; sometimes you will acknowledge your sinfulness and cry for pardon and ask for help. Try to elicit the acts that accord with the pious disposition, the spiritual mood, of the moment.

∞

Meditation leads to
greater knowledge of the Faith

During meditation, you grow in knowledge of your Faith and you acquire principles of right living by applying yourself to prolonged reflection on some doctrine of the Church or teaching of our Savior. You may do this with the aid of a spiritual book or a book of meditations.

But this reflection is only a point of departure for prayer. The more you advance in spiritual ways, the more the work of reasoning is reduced. Prayer is the principal part of every meditation. The subject of meditation provides incentives and matter for prayer. But if it does not lead to conversation with God, it is no longer an internal prayer, but a kind of study or examination of conscience, or a period of spiritual reading for information and enjoyment.

Prayer really begins at the moment when your will, set on fire with love, enters into direct communication with God and yields lovingly to Him in order to please Him and fulfill His precepts and desires. Therefore, the essential element in mental prayer is this contact with God in which you receive the divine life, for the divine life of grace is the source of all holiness.

∞

Prayer dwells essentially in the heart

The Blessed Virgin Mary kept the words of Jesus "in her heart."[93] When our Lord taught His Apostles to pray, He did not bid them apply themselves to reasoning, but to express the love of their hearts as simply as do little children.

As a great theologian, St. Thomas knew that our main avenue of approach to God is love. Although he wrote volumes of deep knowledge of the things of God, he insisted that if we do not love God and His creatures, and our neighbor in Him, and work to increase that love, it matters little how much we know about Him. And Jacques Maritain, a modern theologian, said, "Christianity taught man that love is worth more than intelligence."

St. Teresa of Avila wrote, "It is very advantageous and salutary to occupy oneself during prayer in making acts of praise and of the love of God; to form a desire and a firm purpose to please Him in all things; to rejoice in His goodness because He is sovereign perfection; to wish that all render Him the honor and glory He deserves; to recommend oneself to His mercy; to place oneself simply before Him, admiring His grandeur, humbling oneself at the sight of our miseries; to be indifferent as to what He sends us, be it consolations or dryness, convinced that He knows which is better for us — all these acts tend to

---

[93] Luke 2:51.

fill the mind with holy affections. The great point is not to think much, but to love much."

Endeavor to make acts of love the principal part of your mental prayer. The considerations or reflections are necessary, but only as a means to an end. You may reap more fruit from a simple reading, interspersed with affections and aspirations of the heart, than from an exercise where reason is employed almost exclusively. Reflect or reason only insofar as may be necessary in order to inflame your heart with love and to set your will in motion. St. Jane de Chantal[94] said, "When, in prayer, we find ourselves touched with some holy affections, it is not the time to multiply reflections, but to stop meditation, address oneself to God in words of compunction, of love, of abandonment, according as the inclination may move us. This is the best kind of prayer."

Successful meditation depends above all on a longing for perfection. Use a book only as a means of uniting your heart with God. If you can commune with God only through vocal prayer, then continue vocal prayer. The Holy Spirit has many ways of leading a soul nearer to God. If you are able to speak habitually and simply with God and gain much spiritual food from this communication, do not tie yourself down to any particular methods. Once the best way is found, keep faithfully to it until the Holy Spirit draws you into another way. Be generously docile to His grace.

While meditating, never look for brilliant and striking thoughts or expect to be filled with affections. None of this is

---

[94] St. Jane Frances de Chantal (1572-1641), foundress of the Order of the Visitation.

necessary for spiritual growth. All you need is God's grace. Aim at a sincere, ardent, humble acknowledgment of a plain truth, and consider it a great favor if you attain that much. Be content with what God gives you. Try to assimilate this truth, apply it to yourself, return to it often, and ask God to let it pierce your innermost soul. At the close of your meditation, offer up your good resolutions to God with a firm and resolute promise to keep them faithfully for love of Him. Ask God to help you.

∞

Mental prayer is necessary for
the attainment of perfection

God exhorts us in the Scriptures to meditate on His commandments and to consider His benefits. The consideration in which you engage stirs up your zeal and desire, and thus your prayer gains a fervor that otherwise it would never have. Thereby the effects of prayer — merit, satisfaction, and imperative power — are increased.

In order to reach holiness, you must imitate Jesus Christ. Now, the best source of the knowledge of God and of His nature, His perfections, and His works is the word of Christ contained in the Gospels. There Jesus shows Himself to you in His earthly existence, in His doctrine, and in His love. Christ is God's great Revelation to the world: "This is my beloved Son in whom I am well pleased."[95] If you wish to please the Father, look at His Son and imitate Him. In this is all holiness and salvation: that you be conformed to Jesus Christ.

[95] Matt. 3:17.

Look at Jesus, and contemplate His actions. He does only what is pleasing to His Father. St. Teresa wrote, "Were you at the height of contemplation, take no other road than that of beholding the holy humanity of Jesus. One walks with assurance along that road. Our Lord is for us the source of every good; He Himself will teach us. Look at His life. He is the best Model."

Listen to the words of Jesus, for they are "spirit and life,"[96] as He Himself tells us. They contain life for your soul, not in the manner of the sacraments, but they bear with them the light that enlightens and the strength that sustains. Before He died, Christ expressed the wish that His words abide in you so as to become in you principles of action, and motives of confidence and love. Do not only read the Gospels constantly, but, rather, *pray* the Gospels! It is there that you will find Christ, and, being united to Him by faith, you will bring forth supernatural fruit.

That is why St. Bernard[97] said, "To know Jesus and Him crucified is my philosophy, and there is none higher." And St. Francis de Sales said, "If we would have peace in ourselves, we must have only one single aim and desire, as did St. Paul, who aspired to nothing but to know and to preach our Lord Jesus Christ crucified."

But it is the Holy Spirit who enables you to understand these words of the Gospel in prayerful meditation and all they contain for you. For, before ascending into Heaven, Jesus said, "But the Advocate, the Holy Spirit, whom the Father will

---

[96] John 6:64 (RSV = John 6:63).
[97] Probably St. Bernard (1090-1153), Abbot of Clairvaux. — ED.

send in my name — He will teach you all things and bring to your mind whatever I have said to you."[98] During your meditations on the Gospels, frequently beg the Holy Spirit — the "Finger of God"[99] — to engrave these words on your soul, there ever to remain as a light and principle of action. Then, through the power of prayer and God's grace accompanying it, you will live more and more a Christlike life.

Spiritual reading, combined with reflection and prayer, can become mediation. St. Bernard explains the value of spiritual reading and prayer, and how both should go hand in hand: "Spiritual reading is very necessary to us, for by reading we learn what we must do and what we must shun and to what we must tend. Reading offers to the mind a solid food; meditation masticates and grinds it; prayer contributes to the savor, and contemplation is the very sweetness that delights and strengthens. Thus, by reading we seek the sweetness of a happy life, meditation finds it, prayer asks it, and contemplation tastes it. . . . By prayer — mental and vocal prayer — we are purified from our sins; through reading, we are taught what we should do. Both are good, if possible. If both cannot be had, it is better to pray than to read, for when we pray, we speak with God; when we read, God speaks with us."

∞

Practice mental prayer daily

Always prefer mental to vocal prayer. Even when at vocal prayer, you may put aside the form and follow a higher and

[98] Cf. John 14:26.
[99] Luke 11:20.

more interior uplifting of your heart to God. St. Francis de Sales says, "If you have the gift for mental prayer, always reserve for that the principal place above private vocal prayers."

Mental prayer is best employed after Holy Communion, at visits to the Blessed Sacrament, or with five to ten minutes of spiritual reading before retiring. Remember that it is, after all, the heart that prays. God listens to the voice of the heart, not the lips, and the heart can pray without any words at all.

Try to make at least a short meditation every day. You will find this practice an important means of growing in the love of God. You will gradually acquire the spirit of prayer, which means the habit of having recourse to God more and more frequently.

Adore God for His infinite goodness

We pray, first, to adore God, expressing to Him our love and loyalty. The Holy Bible invites us again and again to give praise and adoration to God in devout prayer — for instance, "Shout with joy to God, all the earth, sing ye a psalm to His name; give glory to His praise. . . . Let all the earth adore Thee and sing to Thee; let it sing a psalm to Thy name."[100]

In Holy Mass, the *Gloria* beautifully expresses the four great acts of prayer: adoration, thanksgiving, reparation, and petition. It begins, "Glory to God in the highest" and later continues, "We worship You, we give You thanks, we praise You for your glory." We delight in thinking of God because He is God, because God is so great and beautiful and holy. Humbly we bow down before Almighty God and promise to serve Him as loving and faithful children. We praise and adore God. That is the first reason we pray.

The angels sing unceasingly in Heaven, "Holy, holy, holy, the Lord God of hosts."[101] In the Old Testament book of Daniel,

---

[100] Ps. 65:1-2, 4 (RSV = Ps. 66:1-2, 4).
[101] Isa. 6:3.

the three young men in the fiery furnace of Babylon sang a beautiful hymn of praise and adoration: "Blessed art Thou, O Lord, the God of our fathers, and Thy name is worthy of praise and glorious forever."[102]

Worship is the paying of homage by religious rites to God. The worship of God is called the worship of adoration. It is the acknowledgment of God's supreme excellence and dominion. We venerate angels and saints, but we worship only God. To Him and to Him alone is adoration due.

Prayer is first and foremost an act of religion, or worship. When you pray, you must acknowledge God's excellence and your total dependence on Him before you ask for anything. Petition is only one of the four ends of prayer, and the other three should accompany and underlie even prayers of petition.

∞

Only God is owed adoration

Adoration is due to God alone, for God alone is supreme. All other beings are creatures, made by God and ruled by Him. Your adoration of God may be purely interior, as when you pray in silence and with your thoughts only. In its strictest sense, worship is an external act, although it must be accompanied by interior devotion. Saying vocal prayers, singing hymns, making the Sign of the Cross, and genuflecting are some of the acts of worship. But if these external acts lack internal devotion, they are merely empty forms.

Official acts of worship, such as the Holy Sacrifice of the Mass, Benediction of the Blessed Sacrament, and certain other

[102] Dan. 3:26.

devotions of the Church, are carried out with prescribed ceremonies called rites.

Worship is not a matter of personal choice or inclination, but an act demanded by the virtue of justice. God has a right to your worship, because He is your supreme Lord and Master. Giving honor to whom honor is due is a requirement of justice. By requiring you, under pain of mortal sin, to attend Mass on Sundays and holy days of obligation, the Church is only insisting on the minimum of worship due to God. But you ought to make it a daily practice to pay to God your tribute of adoration in your prayers, especially in your morning and night prayers.

The whole universe speaks the praise of God. Its very existence is a silent tribute of adoration to the Creator. Storms and waterfalls magnify God's power. The stars and the flowers proclaim His beauty. The laws of nature show forth His wisdom. And the existence of man, surrounded by His goodness, gives proof of His love. But all these things praise God blindly and by force of their natures — all except man himself, whom God endowed with free will. He created man to know, love, adore, and praise Him. From man God asks the love, adoration, and praise that is due Him as Creator. In accomplishing the purpose for which he was made, man finds his highest happiness in time and in eternity.

But God will not force any man to fulfill his destiny. Man is free to refuse God the honor He deserves — and some do refuse. They praise inventors, yet they forget the Creator of all things. They sing their songs to honor great lovers, but they give little or no thought to the Lover of all souls. They write into their histories the names of great benefactors, of fathers of countries, of heroes of the battlefields, but give little thought to their supreme Benefactor, the Father of the universe, or to His Son, who died upon the battlefield of Calvary to conquer evil and win Heaven for all mankind.

The angels, too, praise God gladly. They see Him face-to-face and know how beautiful He is, how strong and tender, how mighty yet merciful, how infinite in His perfections, and how limitless in His love. Their "Holy, holy, holy" rings endlessly throughout Heaven. They find no greater joy than looking upon God's beauty and studying the greatness of His works in deepest wonder and adoration.

∞

Adoration acknowledges
God's dominion over you

Your first and foremost duty is to acknowledge God's supreme dominion over you as your Creator and Father and your absolute dependence on Him as His creature and child. Adoration is the essential act of prayer because it expresses the creature's awareness of the Creator. To adore means to acknowledge your complete dependence upon God, to detach your heart from the passing pleasures of a material world, and to give yourself wholeheartedly back to the God from whom you came. A prayer of adoration sets up the proper relationship between God and the creature made in His image.

Adoration, more than any other act, leads you to acknowledge joyfully the unspeakable richness of the infinitely perfect Being and to accept Him gratefully and reverently as your supreme and soul-satisfying good, the source of all your help in the spiritual and temporal problems of life.

The theological virtues of faith, hope, and charity are tremendous sources of noble thoughts at the moment of union with God in prayer. Faith moves you to profess your belief in Him and in His word, accepting His whole revelation; hope prompts you to affirm your trust in His wisdom and in His goodness, abandoning yourself to His kind Providence; charity inspires you to affirm your love for Him above every other possible object of affection by seeking His will in all things, and by loving your neighbor for His sake.

It may seem as though your adoration, love, and praise of God are imperfect and weak, but you can give Him the greatest adoration, love, and praise possible by offering to Him His own beloved Son in the Mass. You can unite your prayers with Jesus and offer both to God the Father. The strength and warmth of His love and adoration will compensate for the weakness and coldness of yours. Endeavor, then, to join the angels and saints in their adoration of God by being devoted to Holy Mass and to your daily prayers. Do not fail in this happy privilege of adoration.

༄

Consecration of yourself to God
is an ideal prayer of adoration

When you consecrate yourself to God, you fix your attention on God and try to adjust yourself to His will and to give yourself to Him in whatever way He suggests. You offer your daily duties, problems, burdens, trials, misfortunes, inclinations, dangers, joys, and temptations. Believing in Him wholeheartedly, trusting Him absolutely, and loving Him with all your soul, you open your heart completely to God so that He may enter and take possession. And since the Mass is essentially Christ's offering of Himself to the Father, continued and renewed day by day upon the altar, you, as a member of His Mystical Body, unite yourself with Him without reserve, in a union perfected by Holy Communion.

Chapter Eight

∞

Offer thanks to God

We pray, second, to thank God for His favors. In the *Gloria*, we pray, "We give You thanks, we praise You for Your glory." Just as the little dewdrop clinging to a blade of grass or a flower mirrors the splendor and glory of the morning sun, so, too, the heavens and the earth reflect the glory of God the Creator. And for this we thank God.

God's glory shines also in the face of our Savior. We see the glory of God's Son in Jesus' holy life, in His patient sufferings and death, in His glorious Resurrection and Ascension, in His sending of the Holy Spirit, in the institution of the eucharistic sacrifice and the holy sacraments, by which we have received grace after grace. For this, too, we thank God.

The charity of God, sanctifying grace, is also a ray of God's glory; and if we remain faithful, keeping God's grace in our hearts, one day His glory will constitute our eternal happiness. "The charity of God is poured forth in our hearts by the Holy Spirit, who has been given to us."[103] For all these favors we return thanks to God.

[103] Cf. Rom. 5:5.

A loyal Christian is ever grateful for God's innumerable blessings, mindful of the words of St. Paul: "Rejoice always, pray constantly, give thanks in all circumstances, for this is the will of God in Christ Jesus for you."[104]

When Mary visited her cousin Elizabeth, she intoned that glorious canticle the *Magnificat*, in which she praised the mercy, power, and fidelity of God: "My soul magnifies the Lord, and my spirit rejoices in God my Savior. . . ."[105] The priest Zechariah, at the birth of John the Baptist, praised and adored God in the words: "Blessed be the Lord, the God of Israel, because He has visited and wrought the redemption of His people."[106]

∞

Reflection on God's love inspires gratitude

God's purpose in creating the world was not only to give you material goods and security, but also to inspire in you grateful thoughts of Him, so that you might reach your sublime spiritual destiny. Your entire being is God's free gift of love.

He has given you immortality so that you can know, love, and possess Him for all eternity. Through the Redemption, He has raised you to a supernatural plane — that is, He has made you His child, a brother of Jesus, and an heir of Heaven. By His Providence, He watches over you day and night with unfailing care and bestows on you "every best gift."[107] When you wander away from God through sin, He forgives you through

---

[104] 1 Thess. 5:16-18 (RSV).
[105] Luke 1:46-47 (RSV).
[106] Luke 1:68.
[107] James 1:17.

the saving grace of Penance. When you become hungry and tired in soul, He nourishes you with His own Body and Blood. From Baptism to the moment when your eyes, still moist with the strengthening oil of the Anointing of the Sick, are closed in death, He shows you the greatest tenderness and care. How can you reflect on His great love for you and continue to be ungrateful? In your prayers, you can put your gratitude into words.

∞

The Eucharist is an offering of thanksgiving

For all this generosity you have only one fitting return to make: the offering to God of Jesus Christ, His only-begotten Son, in the Mass. Christ has placed this possibility within your hands. The word *Eucharist* means an offering made in thanksgiving. Unite yourself to Jesus, and offer yourself, too, with all that you are and shall do, in thanksgiving for the limitless graces and blessings that have been bestowed upon you. Frequently during the day, as you go about your work, turn your thoughts and affections to God in prayerful gratitude.

∞

Thank God for His countless blessings

Recall the boundless goodness of God to all the world. Yet the world, which enjoys these benefits, forgets to thank its greatest Benefactor. How many Catholics are unfair to God, even on Sunday, by failing to offer God the Mass, this supreme offering of thanksgiving!

To make reparation for the coldness and ingratitude of the many Christians who have no time for prayer or the Sunday observance and to thank God worthily for all the benefits that He has heaped upon an ungrateful world, offer Him His own divine Son in the Mass, for His Son's gratitude is infinitely pleasing in the sight of God and acceptable to Him. Unite your prayers of gratitude to His sublime prayer and to the grateful prayers of the saints, especially to those of the Mother of God, who knew the depths of God's generosity and dedicated her whole life to humble thanksgiving.

You can show your gratitude to God also by being faithful to your morning and night prayers. St. Hippolytus[108] wrote, "Let every faithful man and woman, when they rise from sleep at dawn, before they undertake any work . . . pray to God, and so let them go to their work. Pray also before thy body rests upon thy bed."

There are some Catholics who think it a very small matter to dispense with prayers before and after meals. Not only does this give a bad example to others in the family, especially children, but it also is a sign of coarse ingratitude to God, who gives us the food we eat.

Daniel in the lions' den for six days without food is an example for us. God took pity on His starving servant and commanded an angel to carry Habakuk, with his dish of food, twenty-four hundred miles and place him in the den with Daniel. Daniel did not at once seize the food that God had miraculously sent to him, but first thanked God for His goodness in thinking of him in his need.[109] Daniel thanked God for His blessings. He was grateful even for the food that God has sent

---

[108] St. Hippolytus (c. 170-c. 236), ecclesiastical writer.
[109] Dan. 14:32-38 (RSV = Dan. 14:33-39).

him. He found time to pray, even though he was very hungry. Yet how easily people overlook grace before and after their meals!

∞

Prayer is more than asking
God to grant your requests

Too many people look upon prayer as merely asking God for something. They give little thought to adoration, praise, and thanksgiving, although prayer for these intentions is the most noble and perfect kind of prayer. Prayers of adoration, praise, and thanksgiving will echo throughout Heaven for all eternity. If you really wish to become holy, seek to practice this kind of prayer as perfectly as possible. The result will be God's greater readiness to hear and greater generosity in answering your prayers of petition.

Although the prayer of petition has a place and a definite value in religion, it would be a mistake to confine your prayers merely to asking God for favors.

Many people promise extraordinary things if God will only give them the favor they seek, but once they have received what they want, they forget all about their promise. They get their request, but they pay none of their debts. How many unpaid debts must be written in the account books of God!

We have no record that Christ ever refused a miracle because He knew that people would fail to thank Him. He cured the ten lepers although He was fully aware that only one of them would show gratitude. But He was deeply moved when the one did come back and give thanks for his cure. Jesus remarked, "Were not the ten made clean? But where are the nine? Has no one been found to return and give glory to God except this foreigner?"[110] His gratitude won for the leper the generous praise of Jesus and many spiritual blessings.

Thanksgiving in prayer is frequently overlooked. Our Lord's gentle reproach — "Where are the nine?" — seems like a re-minder for us not to forget the goodness of God. Maybe nine out of ten persons neglect to thank God for blessings received. That, too, may be the ratio between prayers of petition and prayers of thanksgiving. The very thought of the greatness of God's benefits — gifts of soul and body, natural and supernat-ural, known and unknown — would bewilder you if you would take time out to become aware of them.

The realization of being in debt to someone tends to make you humble and brings out the best in you. When that some-one is God, it tends to make you reverent toward Him and, for His sake, generous to your neighbor. The habit of giving thanks seems to develop a sense of stewardship that makes you look upon your possessions as given to you in trust. This view-point, in turn, begets a sense of obligation to repay or at least to account for them.

A powerful motive for thanksgiving is the thought of the many dangers from which you have escaped and the consider-ation that God in His Providence has delivered you from many evils of which you have not even been aware. Most men take for granted not only their freedom from such evils, but all their positive blessings. If you reflect for a moment, you will discover that you are enjoying quite casually a hundred privi-leges that many of your fellow creatures would give anything

[110] Luke 17:18.

to share. You hear and see and walk and are free from acute pain. A visit to a hospital will be more effective than mere reflection.

If you are grateful, you will probably grow more prayerful, for all creatures will remind you of God's goodness. Almost constantly your mind and will can be lifted up to God.

Try to be prompt and grateful in recognizing the blessings of God, for thanksgiving not only meets with God's approval, but gains for you new and greater blessings. St. Teresa of Avila had a very important principle to live by: "In all created things, discern the Providence and wisdom of God, and in all things give Him thanks." Nothing is better calculated to induce a person to continue his favor than gratitude for past benefits. Grateful thanksgiving will dispose us to receive more and more blessings from God. Often think of the many and great gifts that God has bestowed upon you, so that you may excite within yourself valuable sentiments of deep gratitude in loving prayer.

Chapter Nine

∞

Pray to atone for sin

We pray, third, to obtain from God the pardon of our sins and the remission of their punishment. In the *Gloria*, we pray, "Lord Jesus Christ, only Son of the Father, Lord God, Lamb of God, You take away the sins of the world: have mercy on us; You are seated at the right hand of the Father: receive our prayer."

As we recite these words, we should think of the Precious Blood that Christ shed, even to the last drop, for the atonement and the cleansing of all the sins that deluged the world and provoked God's justice. The Son of God took a truly human heart, making it the throne of mercy, allowing it to be opened and pierced with a lance, in order to show mercy and compassion for our weaknesses, wants, and sins. And so we beg God to pardon our sins, to forgive the punishments due to them.

You surely feel the burden of sin, and you long for forgiveness. Only God can deliver you from this crushing weight. In the words of the psalmist you, too, can exclaim, "Evils without number have surrounded me; my iniquities have overtaken me, and I was not able to see. They are multiplied above the hairs of my head, and my heart hath forsaken me. Be pleased, O Lord, to deliver me. Look down, O Lord, to help me."[111]

∞

Prayer helps you atone for and avoid sin

Mortal sin is a grievous offense against God's law. When you break God's law, you hurt God, and that offense against His infinite majesty must be atoned for by penance and prayer.

Sorrow for sin is a fruitful topic of conversation with God. You have only to examine your conscience on the Ten Commandments and the seven deadly sins[112] to realize how greatly you have injured God. If you review the long, sad, shameful history of sin in your past life, you should acknowledge and seek pardon for your sinfulness. The terrifying fact that you have actually offended the all-good and all-holy God should ever keep you in the attitude of the penitent sinner.

St. John Chrysostom offers a most consoling thought: "No matter how great or how numerous the sins may be that we have committed, we should never despair of our salvation nor lose confidence in God, because the divine mercy is infinitely greater than the malice of man." And St. Catherine of Siena[113] advises, "Never consider your past sins except in the light of infinite mercy, so that the memory of them may not discourage you, but may lead you to place your confidence in the infinite value of the Savior's merits."

---

[111] Ps. 39:13-14 (RSV = Ps. 40:12-13).

[112] The seven deadly sins are pride, avarice, envy, wrath, lust, gluttony, and sloth.

[113] St. Catherine of Siena (1347-1380), Dominican tertiary.

You will hardly rise to intimacy with God in prayer without a sincere spirit of compunction. A brief examination of conscience before your morning and night prayers will nourish that spirit. Such a practice will imply that you are setting yourself resolutely to the task of correcting habitual sins, and without this practice, there can be no spiritual progress. Facing the fact that you do have petty sins of pride and unkindness and temper and selfishness, you beg God's forgiveness and promise Him that you will set about the work of improvement and self-discipline. St. Augustine says, "The daily prayers of the faithful make satisfaction for those daily, tiny, light faults from which this life cannot be free."

To make an individual act of contrition will mean more for your spiritual progress than the recitation of long and fine-sounding prayers. A prayer composed by another may outline your guilt and present motives for repentance, yet no one but you can reproduce the exact story of your treachery and measure the depth of your baseness in misusing God's gifts to displease and disobey Him. Your own prayers of contrition best express your sorrow and your humble shame.

Sorrow for sins involves reparation and a purpose of amendment. You wish to repair, as far as possible, the injury that your sin has caused or occasioned — injury to God or to your neighbor. This contrite spirit shows you the need of making reparation for your own sins and for the sins of others by acts of charity and self-denial.

If you are really penitent, you will be concerned also about the danger of falling back into sin, and you will undertake both to shun dangerous occasions and to cultivate a spirit of self-denial.

∞

Jesus has merited forgiveness for your sins

As a wayward child, you have dishonored your heavenly Father by sin, but as your elder Brother and Redeemer, Jesus has atoned for your treachery by His sacrifice on the Cross, now renewed on our altars. Since no action of yours, of itself, is sufficient to win pardon for your sins, you may confidently hope in the merits of your Savior, who in the Mass again offers Himself to win forgiveness for sinners. As on Calvary He re-opened Heaven to sinful mankind, won for penitent sinners release from the danger of Hell, offered to His Father His sufferings and death for those who deserve to suffer and die, and regained for them the love and friendship of God, so in the Mass He again offers Himself for you, a sinner, and for all the sinful world.

Offer the Mass in reparation also for the sins of all mankind. The sinful world that does not pray for itself goes its way of vice and crime gaily and miserably. Men offend God and never ask His forgiveness. Daily they stand in peril of eternal ruin. Through the Mass and also through your prayers of contrition, you can make atonement and obtain for sinners the grace to repent of their sins and to beg forgiveness from God. You can place the consecrated Host as a strong shield between the sinful world and the wrath of God.

As the broken body of Jesus, with His arms outstretched upon the Cross, hung between the sinner and the just vengeance of an offended God, so in the Mass His precious body will stand between us who have sinned, the world that is sinning, and the just anger that should destroy us all. When united with that sacrifice, your own prayers of reparation become limitless in their power to win God's forgiveness and to make reparation.

St. Thérèse of Lisieux[114] expressed confidence in God's mercy with regard to her own soul in the following way: "I have long believed that the Lord is more tender than a mother, and full well do I know more than one maternal heart. I know that a mother is ever ready to forgive the involuntary little failings of her child. I confide to Jesus; I relate to Him in detail my infidelity, thinking, in my daring abandonment, to acquire thus more empire over His heart and to win more fully the love of Him who is not come to call the just, but sinners."

∞

Prayers of contrition please God

It is necessary only to remember the parable of the Pharisee and the publican to see the wonderful power of a prayer of contrition. The Pharisee is the very picture of pride as he stands before God as if he had nothing to ask pardon for. The publican, however, acknowledges his guilt, strikes his breast as a sign of contrition and penance, and says, "O God, be merciful to me a sinner!" God bends in compassion to this humble prayer of reparation and grants His pardon and grace, as the Scripture goes on to show: "This man went back to his home justified rather than the other."[115]

And how touching is that prayer of a model of penitents, St. Augustine, who, in the fourth century, felt the effects of the power of contrite prayer: "Our Father, who hast exhorted

[114] St. Thérèse of Lisieux (1873-1897), Carmelite nun.
[115] Luke 18:9-14.

us to pray, who also bringest about what Thou hast asked of us; since we live better when we pray to Thee and are better: hear me as I tremble in this darkness and reach out Thy hand to me. Hold Thy light before me, and recall me from my strayings, that with Thee as my guide I may return to myself and to Thee. Amen."

Chapter Ten

Ask God for His graces and blessings

We pray, fourth, to ask for graces and blessings for ourselves and others. In the *Gloria*, we are moved by the mercy and kindness of our divine Savior, who has loved us and washed our sins in His Blood. The Lamb of God, who has given Himself as a sacrifice to atone for our sins, will also give us graces and blessings. Therefore, we pray, "Lord Jesus Christ, You take away the sins of the world; receive our prayer." We offer an urgent and earnest petition for grace and pardon, not only for ourselves but also for others, for we say, "Receive our prayer." Our blessed Savior impresses on us all the duty of asking proper gifts of God: "Ask, and it shall be given you; seek and you shall find; knock, and it shall be opened to you."[116]

∞
You depend on God for temporal needs

You need God at every moment of your life in the natural order. Everything you are and have is from God — your body with its senses, your immortal soul with its understanding, free

---

[116] Matt. 7:7.

will, and memory. You cannot so much as preserve the life He has given you without His sustaining help. You may boast that you have intelligence, health, strength, and energy to secure the things you need in life. But your mind and bodily strength are maintained in an active and healthy state by God alone.

The farmer may till the soil and sow the seed, but he cannot make the sun shine or the rain fall in due season. Thus, in every case, we must pray to God to help us in our weakness.

In the Gospels, we see Jesus grant temporal favors in answer to prayer. A leper comes to Him and says, "Jesus, Master, have mercy on me," and Jesus heals him.[117] The people bring to Him a blind man who cries out, "Lord, grant that I may see." Our Lord restores his sight.[118] In the Gospel story of the raising of Lazarus from the dead, Martha went to meet Jesus and said to Him, "Lord, if Thou hadst been here, my brother had not died; but now also I know that whatsoever Thou wilt ask of God, God will give it to Thee." And Jesus said to her, "Thy brother shall rise again."[119] Jesus answered that prayer of faith by one of the greatest of His miracles: restoring life to the dead Lazarus.

In his encyclical letter *On the Mystical Body of Christ*, Pope Pius XII wrote, "There are others who deny any impetratory power to our prayers, or who endeavor to insinuate into men's minds the idea that prayers offered to God in private should be considered of little worth, whereas public prayers which are made in the name of the Church are those which really matter, since they proceed from the Mystical Body of Jesus

[117] Cf. Matt. 8:2-3.
[118] Cf. Mark 10:46-52.
[119] John 11:21-23.

Christ. This opinion is false; for the *divine Redeemer is most closely united not only with His Church, which is His beloved Spouse, but also with each and every one of the faithful, and He ardently desires to speak with them heart to heart, especially after Holy Communion.*

"It is true that public prayer, inasmuch as it is offered by Mother Church, excels any other kind of prayer by reason of her dignity as Spouse of Christ; but *no prayer, even the most private, is lacking its dignity or power, and all prayer is of the greatest help to the Mystical Body* in which, through the Communion of Saints, no good can be done, no virtue practiced by individual members, which does not redound also to the salvation of all.

"Neither is a man forbidden to ask for himself particular favors, even for this life, merely because he is a member of this Body, provided he is always resigned to the divine will; for the members restrain their own personality and remain subject to their own individual needs."[120]

You may ask for temporal as well as for spiritual favors. You must pray for everything, for God wishes to be asked by us for everything, from the highest to the lowest, from Heaven and the Holy Spirit to a piece of bread. God is not bound to give us everything, except as a consequence of prayer.

∞

You depend on God in the supernatural order
Your need for God in the supernatural order is even greater. Goodness tends to communicate itself. God is the limitless source of all good and longs to share this good with others. He

---

[120] *Mystici Corporis Christi*, 89.

has even assured you that your goal is to reign with Him in Heaven and there to share His own happiness forever. To help you secure this glorious goal, He sent His own divine Son to earth to become man and redeem you on the Cross. This same Savior established His Church to guide you, gave her the sacraments to sanctify you, and if anything more is needed, He has given you further assurance that He will answer your prayers. Jesus invites you to ask for His graces and promises to grant them: "Ask and you will receive."

You are, therefore, certain of pleasing God by presenting your requests to Him. You need light to guide you. Who will give it to you if not the Father of light? You need courage and strength to follow the light. Who will give these except the One who is all-powerful? What else can you do but implore the help of Him whose one desire is to help you?

In the Gospels, we see Jesus grant spiritual favors in answer to prayer. Grace itself is granted to prayer. A Samaritan woman asks Him to give her of the living water of which He is the source and which procures eternal life. He reveals Himself to her as the Messiah and leads her to confess her sins in order that He might forgive them.[121] Upon the cross, the good thief asks Him for a remembrance, and He grants him complete forgiveness, even Heaven itself, in the words: "This day thou shalt be with me in Paradise."[122]

---

[121] John 4:7 ff.
[122] Luke 23:42-43.

Part Three

∞

Develop the qualities that make prayer effective

Chapter Eleven

Be humble in prayer

When you say you have prayed in vain, you seem to imply that God has not kept His promise. You blame God, instead of looking into yourself for the failure to obtain your requests. St. James says, "You ask and receive not, because you ask amiss."[123] Your prayer is wanting in some essential quality — that is, you do not ask in the right way for your prayer to be acceptable to God and to be made efficacious.

What are some of these essential qualities that make prayer acceptable to God and efficacious for our salvation? The most important qualities necessary to make our prayer pleasing to God are humility, confidence, sincerity, perseverance, resignation, and attention.

∞

God hears those who pray humbly

Prayer must, first of all, be humble, for it is precisely to keep us mindful of our nothingness, sinfulness, and complete dependence upon Him that God has commanded us to pray.

[123] James 4:3.

Hence, the Holy Scriptures tell us, "God resists the proud, but gives grace to the humble";[124] "The prayer of him that humbles himself shall pierce the clouds . . . and he will not depart till the Most High behold."[125]

Grace is a free gift of God to which you have no right whatsoever. You have no claims on God's justice, but must confidently rely on His mercy. God knows your needs before you ask, better than you do yourself, and He does not need to be informed of them. But He wants you to ask for them in order that, through prayer, you may be made aware of your utter dependence on Him for all and that you may be reminded of His goodness to you.

When you pray, you must be aware of your nothingness in the sight of God, of your utter dependence on His goodness, of the immense difference between you who ask and God who grants. Try to realize your unworthiness, your insignificance, and God's infinite condescension in listening to you, a sinful creature.

Abraham considered himself but dust and ashes in the presence of the divine Majesty: "I will speak to my Lord, whereas I am dust and ashes."[126] When he prayed for the deliverance of the Jewish people, Daniel did not rely on his own merits and virtues, but on God's mercy. "It is not for our justifications that we present our prayers before Thy face, but for the multitude of Thy tender mercies."[127]

[124] Cf. James 4:6.
[125] Ecclus. 35:21.
[126] Gen. 18:27.
[127] Dan. 9:18.

The publican in the Gospel prayed with humility and was heard. "Standing afar off, he would not so much as lift up his eyes to Heaven, but kept striking his breast, saying, 'O God, be merciful to me a sinner!' " And Jesus said, "I tell you, this man went back to his home justified rather than the other; because everyone who exalts himself shall be humbled, and he who humbles himself shall be exalted."[128]

In the Gospel, a centurion came to Jesus, beseeching Him to cure his servant who was "sick of the palsy and grievously tormented." Jesus promised to come and heal the servant. But the centurion, in his humility, made answer in those memorable words that express his humble confession of unworthiness: "Lord, I am not worthy that Thou shouldst enter under my roof. Say but the word, and my servant shall be healed." There is both humility and confidence shown in his petition: humility, because he realized his unworthiness; confidence, since he believed it sufficient for our Lord merely to speak the word. Our Lord rewarded the humility and faith of the centurion by telling him, "Go, and as thou hast believed, so be it done to thee." The Gospel narrator closes the episode in these simple words: "And the servant was healed at the same hour."[129]

The proud man attributes the effects of his prayer to himself, while the humble man attributes them to God. Would you expect God to hear you just to flatter your self-love? If you are humble, you will sincerely admit that all you have is from God, and hence God, in listening to your prayer, procures His own glory as well as your welfare.

[128] Cf. Luke 18:13-14.
[129] Matt. 8:5-13.

The prayers of children are powerful, because they pray with humility. We, too, must pray with the simplicity and humility of children, for Jesus taught us to pray, "Our Father." And Jesus said, "Amen I say to you, unless you be converted and become as little children, you will not enter into the kingdom of Heaven."[130]

---

[130] Matt. 18:3.

Chapter Twelve

Pray with confidence

The second quality of prayer is confidence, for by this we give glory to the power, goodness, and fidelity of God.

Prayer is the expression of your desire before God. This desire arises from wanting something that you are unable to procure. When you pray, you recognize God as being in a position to grant your petitions. He can be trusted to bestow on you all that you need for the attainment of life's purpose. Having created you for a supernatural destiny   for the happiness proper to Himself — He, by this very fact, undertakes to give you all that is required for gaining that happiness. In His generosity, He usually does not content Himself with giving what is sufficient by way of means, but very often He gives most abundantly. But He cannot be expected to answer your requests when they do not bear on what makes for a good life, as God understands a good life.

∞

Scripture exemplifies confident prayer
Throughout Old Testament history, God is represented as the Father of mankind. Abraham had sufficient confidence in

God to carry out to the extreme limit, even at peril of his son's life, his heavenly Father's commands to him.[131] The Scriptures say, "He is the protector of all that trust in Him";[132] "Blessed is the man that trusteth in Thee."[133]

In the New Testament especially, we are encouraged to pray with confidence. Our Lord uses the most compelling words and the most touching parables. "If one of you asks his father for a loaf, will he hand him a stone? Or for a fish, will he . . . hand him a serpent? Or if he asks for an egg, will he hand him a scorpion? Therefore, if you, evil as you are, know how to give good gifts to your children, how much more will your heavenly Father give the Holy Spirit to those who ask Him!"[134]

In the Gospel is the incident of the blind man who sat by the road, begging. Hearing that Jesus of Nazareth was passing by, the blind man began to cry, "Jesus, son of David, have mercy on me!" The companions of Jesus rebuked him and bade him be silent. But his trust in Jesus was so great that he cried the louder until Jesus heard him and commanded that he be brought near. "And when he drew near, He asked him saying, 'What wouldst thou have me do for thee?' And he said, 'Lord, that I may see.' And Jesus cured his blindness, saying, 'Thy faith has saved thee.' "[135]

Another time, Jesus said, "Have faith in God. Amen I say to you, whoever says to this mountain, 'Arise, and hurl thyself

---

[131] Cf. Gen. 22:1 ff.
[132] Ps. 17:31 (RSV = Ps. 18:30).
[133] Ps. 83:13 (RSV = Ps. 84:12).
[134] Luke 11:11-13.
[135] Luke 18:35-42.

into the sea,' and does not waver in his heart, but believes that whatever he says will be done, it shall be done for him. Therefore I say to you, all things whatever you ask for in prayer, believe that you shall receive, and they shall come to you."[136]

At the Last Supper, Jesus solemnly promised an answer to prayer when He said, "Whatever you ask in my name, that I will do, in order that the Father may be glorified in the Son. If you ask me anything in my name, I will do it."[137] Later, He said, "In that day, you shall ask in my name, and I do not say to you that I will ask the Father for you, for the Father Himself loves you because you have loved me."[138]

&

Confidence makes prayer fruitful

Christ gave us a definite promise. But it is also a command to make use of prayer to obtain favors or necessities. God is faithful to His promises, and He will grant an answer to prayer.

Not to have wholehearted trust in prayer would amount to doubting God and His promises. It is like underrating the merits of Jesus Christ and His all-powerful prayer as our Mediator before the Father.

Without faith and confidence, prayer is fruitless. Some have so little confidence that if they do not receive an answer to their prayer at once, they give up hope and discontinue their prayers. St. James says, "But if any of you is wanting in wisdom, let him ask it of God, who gives abundantly to all

[136] Mark 11:23-24.
[137] John 14:13.
[138] John 16:26-27.

men, and does not reproach; and it will be given to him. But let him ask with faith, without hesitation. For he who hesitates is like a wave of the sea, driven and carried about by the wind. Therefore, let not such a one think that he will receive anything from the Lord, being a double-minded man, unstable in all his ways."[139] And St. Paul admonishes, "Let us, then, with confidence draw near to the throne of grace, that we may receive mercy and find grace to help in time of need."[140]

Do not wish to settle the time and manner of having your request granted. Do not tell God what He ought to do, but, rather, seek humbly the favor you need.

∞

The thought of God's goodness and power
will give you confidence in prayer

God is eternally the same. When you appeal to Him with the right intention and with sincerity, He answers your petitions. No prayer remains unanswered if offered with faith, humility, perseverance, and resignation to God's will. He does not always grant you what you ask or in the manner you expect it, but He always grants that which is best for you in eternity.

If you expect your petitions to be answered, you must go to prayer convinced that God will hear you. Imagine a man approaching a friend and saying, "I'm going to ask you to do this for me, but I realize it's just a waste of time. I know you won't do it for me, but I'll take a chance anyway." The friend would be insulted and would certainly not grant the favor. Such an

---

[139] James 1:5-8.
[140] Heb. 4:16 (RSV).

approach to God is not at all uncommon. People say, "God, I'm asking You for this, but I hardly expect to get it. Maybe You'll give it to me, but I'm not too hopeful." In that case, it would be a miracle if God did work against our lack of faith and confidence. Even Christ did not perform His miracles for people who had no faith. In the Gospel, we find that in certain places He did no healing "because of their lack of faith."[141] God can hardly be expected to answer the prayer of a person who really does not believe that He answers prayer.

With years in the practice of your religion, there will grow a deepened belief in the power of prayer. At first, you accept on faith the promise that whatsoever you ask will be given to you. Gradually you get to feel that it is a truth you can prove from experience. Prayer is infallibly answered; that is all there is to it. People pray, and God listens. They place their requests at God's feet, and He grants them.

Life can be a success in all the finest senses of the word, because, if you pray, God will be on your side. Prayer is the invisible power that will make you stronger than the strongest of your enemies. But the full power of prayer can be made to serve you only if you have confidence in God, who can help you because He is almighty and who wants to help you because He is goodness itself.

---

[141] Cf. Mark 6:5-6.

Chapter Thirteen

∞

Pray with a sincere heart

The third quality of prayer is sincerity. On Good Friday, when Jesus was nailed to the Cross, two thieves were crucified with Him, one on His right and one on His left. A great crowd stood around the three crosses. The people mocked Jesus. Even the chief priests with the scribes and the elders said, "He saved others; Himself He cannot save. If He be the King of Israel, let Him now come down from the Cross, and we will believe in Him."[142] One of the thieves crucified with Jesus also mocked Him and cried out, "If Thou be Christ, save Thyself and us!" But the other thief rebuked his companion and said, "Neither dost thou fear God, seeing thou art under the same condemnation? And we indeed justly, for we receive the due reward of our deeds; but this man hath done no evil." Turning to Jesus, he said, "Lord, remember me when Thou shalt come into Thy kingdom." And Jesus said to him, "Amen, I say to thee, this day thou shalt be with me in Paradise."[143] What a generous answer to a sincere prayer that came forth from the

[142] Matt. 27:42.
[143] Luke 23:39-42.

heart of a repentant sinner! How insincere the prayer of the other thief!

∞

You must sincerely want
the things for which you pray

People are sometimes not sincere, for instance, when they pray to be delivered from an insistent temptation. They do not really want the thing they pray for, because they may be quite fond of the temptation.

If you are not interested enough to make some effort toward getting the thing you ask for, you really do not want it. God would be delighted to bring about a conversion if He saw you doing something to help bring the conversion about. He would give real light in examinations if He saw you making serious efforts to master the subject. He would be happy to crown with success an enterprise in which He saw you taking enough interest to work hard and use the ordinary means that are necessary to promote its success.

You prove that you want a thing by using the normal means of getting it. God will cooperate with you if you combine effort with prayer. God will not work miracles if you decline work and put the whole burden on His shoulders.

The reason some of your prayers are not answered is because you make use of prayer to ask for needless graces — graces according to your taste. For instance, you pray for the grace of sanctification — graces for the future, not for the present; graces that would do away with all difficulties, that would leave no room for effort. You are asking for miraculous graces that would accomplish great things, graces that would change the whole order of Providence, not those that would only help you to walk.

When you ask Christ to cooperate with you in gaining a request, you must regard the request as something important, something that is close to the Heart of the Savior. Jesus wants all that concerns human happiness and the salvation of souls. The peace and joy of His followers, their health and prosperity, insofar as these do not interfere with their eternal destiny, are His concern. The girl who prays that Christ may safeguard her from sinning or being the occasion of sin to anyone is praying according to the Heart of Christ. But she is not praying according to the Heart of Christ if she asks God not to permit an impure relation to be broken up or to prosper a love affair that is far from honorable. A woman should not pray for a beautiful home because she has grown fiercely jealous of her neighbor's home. A man should not pray for a better job merely to satisfy his ambition. God can hardly be expected to further our vanities and our selfish ambitions. He would be a poor sort of a father if He did!

Some people pray to God for things that are wrong and sinful. They may ask God to bless with success a dishonest business deal or a shady enterprise. When people ask God for things they do not need, or cannot really use, they are imposing on His goodness. Selfishness, self-seeking, petty greed, and vanity can inspire a great many of the requests that send us running prayerfully to God. That is why St. John of Damascus[144] says, "Prayer is a raising up of the mind to God or a petitioning of God for what is fitting."

---

[144] St. John of Damascus (c. 675-c. 749), Greek theologian.

Chapter Fourteen

∞

Persevere in your prayer

The fourth quality of prayer is perseverance, for we never cease to be dependent upon God's help. Therefore we should continually ask for it. Some favors God grants, not the first time we pray for them, but only after repeated requests. Our Lord, therefore, has told us, "Watch, then, praying at all times, that you may be accounted worthy to escape all these things that are to be, and to stand before the Son of Man."[145] St. Paul says, "Continue steadfastly in prayer, being watchful in it with thanksgiving."[146]

Confidence is tested by perseverance. Some people stop praying when they do not get what they ask for immediately. They fail in that perseverance which is the test of real faith and confidence. Persistence is rewarded among men. Our Lord suggests that it is even influential with God. When St. Augustine was steeped in heresy, St. Monica[147] prayed for more than twenty years for his conversion. Her request seemed worthy of

[145] Luke 21:36.
[146] Col. 4:2.
[147] St. Monica (c. 331-387), mother of St. Augustine.

an immediate answer. But God tested the confidence and perseverance of this mother first and then granted her petition a hundredfold.

Our Lord once told this parable: "Which of you shall have a friend and shall go to him in the middle of the night and say to him, 'Friend, lend me three loaves, for a friend of mine has just arrived on a journey, and I have nothing to set before him'; and he will answer from within, 'Do not bother me; the door is now shut, and my children are with me in bed; I cannot get up and give you anything.' I tell you, though he will not get up and give him anything because he is his friend, yet because of his importunity, he will rise and give him whatever he needs."[148] The argument is plain: if a man will finally yield to persistence, not because he is a friend, but to avoid the very annoyance of being asked over and over again, how much more will God, who is our loving Father, yield to persistence in our prayers?

We know that God always hears our prayers if we pray properly because our Lord has promised, "If you ask the Father anything in my name, He will give it to you."

Perseverance has a special power of obtaining what is asked, because it presupposes humility, earnest will, and ardent desire, as Jesus said, "Yet because of his persistence he will get up and give him all he needs." Like the man at his friend's door, you ought to call, entreat, knock, and allow our Lord no peace until He grants your prayer.

Scripture says that Jesus related the parable of the unjust judge and the widow to show them "that they must always

[148] Luke 11:5-8 (RSV).

pray and not lose heart."[149] One does "always" what one does much and often, and never ceases to do. By His own promise, God has pledged Himself, His goodness, and His justice to hear persevering prayer. God cannot resist persevering prayer. A promise is given to this perseverance: "Ask and it shall be given to you."[150]

Perseverance in prayer is even more strikingly brought out in the Scripture story of a pagan woman. Our Lord undertook a journey with His disciples into the Gentile land of Tyre and Sidon. A Gentile woman came to Him and followed Him, imploring Him to deliver her daughter who was possessed by a devil and grievously troubled. Our Lord paid no attention to her entreaties and answered the Apostles, as they interceded for her, that He was sent only to the sheep of the house of Israel who were lost. No trials were able to make this woman waver in her confidence. Our Lord never put anyone else to such a hard test. First, He let her follow and entreat Him all along the street, without even looking at her. Yet she hurried after Him, fell at His feet, and said, "Lord, help me!" Jesus replied: "It is not fair to take the children's bread and to cast it to the dogs." But she said, "Yes, Lord, yet even the dogs eat the crumbs that fall from their master's table." The Jews looked upon the pagans as dogs, and Jesus used this harsh term to test the faith of this woman. Jesus answered, " 'O woman, great is your faith! Be it done for you as you desire.' And her daughter was healed from that moment."[151]

---

[149] Luke 18:1.

[150] Matt. 7:7.

[151] Matt. 15:21-28 (RSV).

It is really a blessing to be given an opportunity to practice perseverance, to cooperate earnestly with grace, and to be purified, tried, and humbled. In this manner, we prepare ourselves best for the reception of great graces.

Do not become discouraged if God delays in answering your prayers. He has reasons for His delay. God may wish to strengthen your faith and to cleanse your soul more fully. Humble yourself the more, believe more firmly, and cleanse your heart more completely from earthly attachments. God is most generous, kind, and good. He knows all things and chooses what is for your greater good. When the right time comes, He will in His mercy grant you the graces you need.

When you make a novena — that is, a devotion lasting nine days — you exercise perseverance, which Jesus encouraged. Before our Lord ascended into Heaven, He told His Apostles and disciples and His Mother to go to Jerusalem and prepare themselves for the coming of the Holy Spirit. They persevered in prayer for nine days. On the tenth day — Pentecost — the Holy Spirit came upon them.[152] This was the Church's first novena.

However, superstition sometimes creeps into the lives of very good people. They hear somewhere that if you say a certain prayer for so many days, or if you say it in a certain way every night, you will get whatever you ask. It is not essentially a matter of prayer, they tell you, but a particular prayer. To them, the quality of the prayer, its faith and intensity, is not important, but its quantity is essential. They consider prayer a kind of magic formula.

[152] Acts 1:4, 12-14; 2:1-4.

God never promised that He would answer a petition just because it was backed by a certain prayer, however lovely, said a definite number of times. There is no magic charm attached to a formula that is repeated a certain number of times. There are prayers so worded, either by Christ Himself or the Church or holy men, that they powerfully and beautifully present our needs to God. They say eloquently what we ourselves might say falteringly. The repetition of these prayers is efficacious, not because some mysterious power comes from using them a certain number of times, but because each time they are said, the petition is expressed forcefully and with a deepening impression on the person who makes it. Repetition follows our Lord's advice to persevere in prayer.

But it is the intensity of the spirit behind the prayer and the perseverance in it that matters. A prayer of petition may be said only once and yet be said with such faith and desire that it is sufficient to move the heart of God. A formula may be thoughtlessly repeated a hundred times without any effect whatsoever. Prayer must be said with faith, confidence, perseverance, and a remembrance that we are calling in, as our intercessor, Jesus Christ, in whose name prayer must be recited if it is to be fruitful.

It is good to know on the testimony of Jesus that His heavenly Father never grows weary of listening to your petitions. He may refuse your request, not because He does not love you, but because He has good reason for delaying the granting of your petition, or because He desires that you should ask it more urgently.

Do not stop praying if the answer to your prayers is long delayed. You must be prepared to be tried and tested, to be kept waiting until God sees fit to give what you ask. Unless you persevere in your prayer, you may expect disappointment. God has the right to demand faith and confidence, to test you by your perseverance, and to grant your petition when and where and how He chooses. His way will always be to your best advantage.

Submissively adore the wisdom of God if He withholds altogether the favor you implore. Knock at God's door confidently, and ask trustfully; but leave to Him the time and manner of the answer. He will give you either the thing you ask for or something else that, in eternity, you will recognize to be immeasurably better. He wants to help you, because He is all-good; He knows how to help you, because He is all-wise; He can help you, because He is all-powerful.

Chapter Fifteen

∽

Abandon yourself to God's will

The fifth quality of prayer is resignation. In order to be truly efficacious, prayer must be directed to things conducive to salvation, for God looks at all things from the viewpoint of eternity, and He will not give us anything that would prejudice our eternal welfare. Too often, in our shortsightedness, we ask only for temporal favors, some of which would not be good for us. When, therefore, we pray for such temporal things, we should be careful to add, "If it be Your holy will." We can ask for spiritual favors without reserve. In other words, we should pray with resignation to God's holy will.

One day, a leper came and adored Jesus, saying, "Lord, if Thou wilt, Thou canst make me clean."[153] He had probably heard of the goodness and miraculous power of Jesus, and so he took courage to push his way to His side, although this was forbidden by the law. He had an extraordinary degree of faith and confidence in the power and goodness of Jesus.

The leper came to Jesus with the greatest confidence that, since He was the Son of God, vested with all power over

[153] Matt. 8:2.

creation, He could grant his petition if He willed to. It was only a question of whether He wanted to. He was resigned to the will of God in regard to the restoration of his health.

Our Lord gave a special sign of His compassion and kindness by touching the loathsome sufferer with His hand and thus effected a cure. Jesus then said, "I will. Be thou made clean."[154] He was pleased with the faith, and especially with the resignation, of the sick man, who had left all to the decision of the Master.

∞

Strive to accept God's will

By resignation you express your readiness to make God's will your own. You will not desire anything but what He offers; you will not object to anything that He permits. You will follow any course of action that may be outlined in His plan for you. Through this surrender, you pay Him a supreme tribute of love and adoration.

Three principles are the basis of the virtue of resignation, or abandonment: nothing can ever happen without the permission of God; whatever God permits will ultimately be fitted into His plan; in that plan, man's best interests are inseparable from the interests of God.

With these principles in mind, you readily come to the conclusion that you have nothing to fear except the danger of not being sufficiently submissive to God. Therefore, do all you can to further His will so far as it is clear to you, and having done this, abandon yourself completely to whatever may happen.

[154] Matt. 8:3.

Fortitude is the cardinal virtue that disposes us to do what is good in spite of any difficulty. And out of faith and humble prayer grow determination and fortitude. And yet in all trials, one must be entirely resigned to God's holy will.

Patience is a form of fortitude that enables you to do the will of God, whatever it may cost. St. Francis de Sales put it this way: "We must have patience not only to be ill, but to be ill with the illness which God wills, in the place where he wills, and among such persons as He wills; and so of other tribulations."

Sanctity cannot be anything else but the perfect and complete fulfillment of the will of God, and there can be nothing more perfect than that. Doing His holy will is our first and greatest duty.

It takes heroic courage to realize this ideal of abandonment to the will of God, although it is a very simple ideal of holiness and a necessary condition for spiritual progress. To recognize with joy the absolute supremacy of God's will and to embrace it with gladness and utter unselfishness is to pray in a manner that is most sublime and spiritually fruitful.

The prayer of resignation can be practiced in innumerable incidents of your daily life. Bad weather, an unwelcome visitor, a disappointment, sickness, delays, accidents, a neighbor's rudeness — all these are providential opportunities to turn to God in a prayer of resignation.

∞

Pray for what leads to everlasting life
The most important condition to make your prayer effective is to ask for those things that lead to everlasting life: for

supernatural graces, first of all, and then for temporal goods, insofar as they may help you to save your soul. This rule was laid down by our Lord Himself: "Therefore do not be anxious, saying, 'What shall we eat?' or, 'What shall we drink?' or, 'What are we to put on?' for your Father knows that you need all these things. But seek first the kingdom of God and His justice, and all these things shall be given you besides."[155]

It is right and proper to ask God for gifts, just as it is for children to ask their father for what they need, or think they need; and the father is pleased if the children trustfully ask him. This holds true even for material needs, for Jesus taught us to ask, "Give us this day our daily bread."[156]

However, it is important to note that requests are not the only, nor are they the first, items of the Lord's Prayer. The request for daily bread comes in the fourth place, after we have already given due praise and worship to God and exalted His name, His kingdom, and His will.

Your happiness and holiness consist in having God, and prayer is the means necessary to reach Him. Do not ask for anything that is not in harmony with the will of God.

∞

God will supply your needs,
but not always your wants

Temporal goods in themselves are not enough to satisfy the craving of your heart for happiness. But you need certain temporal goods in order to live and to secure your salvation. You

[155] Matt. 6:31-33.
[156] Matt. 6:11 (RSV).

are therefore allowed to ask for them insofar as they may help you save your soul.

What is necessary to reach the goal of your existence are your needs. Your wants and longings may have no important connection with what is required to attain your final end. It is possible for your wants to extend far beyond your needs. God always consults your interests and wills your happiness, but does not indulge your fancies. His love for you would not permit Him to grant what might bring harm to your soul.

To pray successfully, you must have a clear idea of what you need, as distinct from what you want. Your wants are mainly of your own making, but your needs are natural and of God's creation. You have but one need, and that need is God. "All our prayers," says St. Thomas, "ought to be directed to the obtaining of grace and glory."[157] That which in your prayers is not heard is what proceeds from yourself and self-love. "The cause of our prayer," St. Thomas continues, "ought to be the longing desire for divine love, and it is from it that our prayer should proceed. It abides virtually in everything we do for the love of God. 'In everything,' as the apostle writes to the Corinthians, 'we ought to act in view of our procuring the glory of God.' It is in this way that our prayers must be unremitting."[158] It is not the desire of uniting yourself more closely to God by love, but the longing for what will make your life on earth more agreeable, that moves you to ask for certain requests. If the desire to find God is not included in your petition, the principal condition of successful prayer is wanting.

[157] *Summa Theologica*, II-II, Q. 83, art. 4.
[158] Ibid., art. 14.

Therefore, you should pray with full confidence for the things that cannot possibly turn to your disadvantage. Ask only conditionally for those things that can prove either a help or a hindrance according to the use you make of them. This means praying for created things in a way that is acceptable to God, adjusting your attitude in these things to that of the Holy Spirit who guides you.

It is quite legitimate to ask the Lord for all that is required to lead a truly human life. Hence, the temporal needs we pray for must have a connection with the obtaining of grace and glory. Do not seek temporal things for themselves. Temporal things must be sought only as a means to a good life. St. Thomas says, "We may ask God to grant us temporal things insofar as they are expedient to our salvation."[159]

God alone knows what will work in favor of your sanctification and what will prove harmful to it. You are a poor judge in the matter. What you ask for must be of benefit to your soul, or at least not harmful to salvation, and this you cannot always judge. God, who is all-knowing, may foresee evil results in the granting of your petition in the way you wish it. St. Prosper of Aquitaine,[160] who lived in the fifth century, wrote, "He who asks of God, in faith, things needful for this life is sometimes mercifully heard and sometimes mercifully not heard. For the Physician knows better than the patient what will avail the sick man."

The mother of the sons of Zebedee came to our Lord with the prayer, "Command that these my two sons may sit, one at

---

[159] Ibid., art. 6.

[160] St. Prosper of Aquitaine (c. 390-c. 463), theologian.

Thy right hand and one at Thy left hand, in Thy kingdom."
Our Lord answered, "You do not know what you are asking
for."[161] She was hoping to obtain good positions for her sons in
an earthly kingdom, ignorant of the fact that our Lord was
speaking of a spiritual kingdom. So, too, we often ask for things
of which we do not understand all the possible consequences
to ourselves.

Will a mother give a sharp knife to her child to play with,
simply because the glitter of the blade attracts him?

A sick person may plead to be restored to health, and it
seems to be a reasonable request. But maybe God foresees that
health will bring with it forgetfulness of religion and of Him,
and result in the possible loss of a soul. In reality, the prayer is
answered in a far better way — God may grant the gift of patience or resignation to suffering, which is more beneficial to
the soul.

As a kind and loving Father, God is deeply interested in
seeing that your life should be truly happy, and He is eager to
give you every help to make it successful. But it too frequently
happens that His view and your view of what success in life really means do not agree. Do not be a routine Christian who
may have faith enough to know and to acknowledge that life is
meant to be the pursuit of God, but would still make Him one
among many other pursuits. God cannot be expected to adjust
Himself to an outlook that has no relation to your spiritual interests. It is true that God is not indifferent to the things of
human life, but they are valued by Him only insofar as they
serve man in his progress toward eternal life.

---

[161] Matt. 20:21-22.

We often pray to God for things that we believe to be good and useful, but which would be ruinous for us. For that reason, God often refuses to give us the things for which we pray. He refuses because He loves us. Sometimes He permits us to suffer so that we may draw closer to Him. Therefore, we must pray with loving trust in His goodness because, as our God and Father, He knows what is best for us.

∞

God hears prayers that spring from grace

God never turns a deaf ear to prayer that has its origin in grace and not in natural inclinations. When prompted by the Holy Spirit, prayer will in all cases interpret before God your soul's true needs. But even when your desires do not spring from selfish motives, and what you ask of God is undeniably good, as in the case of a virtue to be acquired or a vice to be overcome, it may be that your request is not granted because you are wanting in the proper dispositions — namely, humility, perseverance, and constancy.

Even when it is a question of a particular grace, ask for it only on the condition that it is the will of God that you have it. God in His infinite wisdom knows better than you do what is suitable for your soul. You must desire your salvation according to God's own way and desire such graces as He grants to you. You must hold on to the graces He grants you, for your will must harmonize with His.

Remember that nothing happens aimlessly; everything comes from a good Providence. Think and judge all things in terms of the inner life of prayer. Weather, achievements, misfortunes, sufferings, wars — all these are to be referred to God, with the firm conviction that everything must have something of God's goodness in it. Judge all things in terms of the divine.

God frequently makes deliverance from evil depend upon our prayers. The way to overcome evil in the world is not to complain about it or blame God or the Church for it, but to pray that God may deliver us from it.

In all the circumstances of life, always say, "Thy will be done," with all your heart. God loves you, and what He sends or permits is for your own good. Perhaps only in eternity will you see the masterpiece of His plan and understand it.

God watches over you in loving care even in the sufferings of life just as He loved you when He allowed His Son to die for your soul. He dispenses His graces, giving consolation or suffering, peace or struggle, according to the designs of His wisdom and the needs of your soul. You have only to leave in His hands the choice of the graces that will prove most beneficial to you. Certainly, you may express a wish, but do it in humble submission to the will of your heavenly Father. He will always answer your prayer if you ask as you ought. If at times He gives you, in place of what you ask, something greater and better, it is your place to thank Him rather than complain.

In all your prayers, there should be a certain longing that God should replace self in you and substitute His life for your own. As a true Christian, endeavor to make your spiritual effort consist in cultivating the desire of God and gradually eliminating all desires that are not of Him. Be constantly conscious of your continual and necessary dependence on God, in each detail of your life. Because of our fallen state, nothing can prevent us from falling into sin except the continual grace of

God. You must always ask for it and constantly be aware of your need of it.

For beginners in the spiritual life, prayer to God for aid in the struggle against what is corrupt in them — that is, their evil tendencies and habits — is a necessity. For those who are progressing in the spiritual life, prayer to God should be directed to this end: that their actions should be morally correct and as fully as possible animated by divine love. They should ask God to fill their life and actions with grace each day and to grant them temporal things only insofar as these favor growth in the divine life.

∞

God shows His goodness in
not granting your every wish

How fortunate for you that God does not always give you what you ask for. You would indeed be in the worst possible position if you could control what comes to you along life's way. You cannot see the future. You have no real way of knowing what is going to be for your good. When it comes to picking things for yourself, how badly you sometimes choose and how mistakenly you plan. On the other hand, the thing you did not want or plan or expect may be exactly the blessing that makes you wonderfully happy and fortunate.

God sees the future. When you lay a request at His feet, He might be quite cruel if He granted it. The man on whom a young woman has set her heart might, if she married him, turn out to be the very person who would wreck her life. Health at a certain moment may seem very important. Yet sickness may be, and usually is, the blessing that crowns life with its richest achievements. Wealth or success may sometimes bless a life, but there are times when, if it were given in answer to prayer, either wealth or success would ruin a life, spoil a home, or destroy a family.

You are so completely ignorant of the future that you often pray for the success of someone who, if your prayer were answered in the manner you desire, would be thereby doomed to lifelong misery and maybe eternal failure. You may be asking for what would be the worst thing you could possibly have. Not all things that appear good to you are worth having. Since you do not always know what is good for you, leave the answer to your prayers to God. He knows best because He knows the future and He loves you more than anyone else can.

∽

You cannot always see the results of your prayers

God does not always let you see the results of your prayers. Praying is not like putting a coin into a slot and getting the article you want. God tests your faith. He does not always answer your prayers visibly. People may die without any sign of conversion. The prayers for their conversion are not lost. We shall find that out in eternity. Of course, God cannot force a person's conversion; everyone has to use his own free will. But you can be absolutely sure that the person receives grace and that God has cared for his soul. Your act of confidence in God is the beautiful tribute of a child to the Father, whose word he accepts even when he has, as in this case, no clear proof that the word has been carried out.

Prayer is never wasted, never lost, if it is said with the proper dispositions of heart.

∽

Pray with resignation to God's will

Let God decide whether your request is suitable or not. "Not my will, but Thine be done" must always be the spirit of your prayer.

Jesus prayed, "Father, if Thou art willing, remove this cup from me." What would have happened to us if that petition had been granted? But Jesus added, "Nevertheless not my will, but Thine be done." Then an angel came to give Him the strength to endure for our sakes the terrible sufferings of the Passion and death on the Cross.[162] That was the answer to His prayer.

Every prayer should be offered in the name and spirit of Jesus. It should be modeled upon His prayer in Gethsemane: "Not my will, but Thine be done." You may be tempted to insist upon the fulfillment of your wishes by God. No matter how good your reasons for departing from the spirit of the Lord's Prayer may be, they will never avail to prove that you know better than God what is best for you, or for your neighbor, or whether your aim is superior to His divine purpose.

You may not get what you ask in the way you want it when you pray, but your prayer is not in vain, since your soul receives something of greater value.

When your prayer seems to remain unanswered, you may find that all desire for what you wanted passes away to be replaced by a desire for something more wholesome. That, too, is an answer to your prayer. Therefore, when you pray, it should always be with the determination to leave to God the

---

[162] Luke 22:42-43 (RSV).

decision as to whether it is good for you to have such a request granted or to have some other more suitable gift.

If you do not always obtain what you pray for, it is either because you have not prayed properly or because God knows that what you are asking for would not be for the good of your soul. Your prayers will be answered not your way, but God's way, for His way is always the best way. He knows better than you what is best for you.

Chapter Sixteen

Be attentive in your prayer

The sixth quality of prayer is attention. Since prayer is a con-versation with God, it should be performed with attention. Merely to pronounce a certain form of words is not prayer. Our Lord once quoted the prophecy of Isaiah when he spoke to the scribes and Pharisees: "This people honors me with their lips, but their heart is far from me."[163]

In speaking with people, it is a matter of courtesy to be attentive to what you are saying. You may not always give the same attention to God. You cannot prevent distractions from creeping into your prayers, but when these are willfully permitted to occupy your attention during prayer, they are discourtesy to God.

∞

Prepare yourself for prayer
It is not easy to keep your attention fixed on unseen objects. This is why your mind may wander and you may become distracted. If you wish to pray with attention, you must prepare

---

[163] Isa. 29:13; Matt. 15:8 (RSV).

for prayer by collecting your thoughts. "Before prayer, prepare thy soul; and be not as a man that tempteth God."[164]

Preparation for prayer is important because of the distractions and selfish interests that make up the routine of everyday living. Before your prayers, you should, as far as possible, banish all worldly thoughts, and picture Almighty God as vividly as you can. At the same time, you ought to think, "Almighty God is here. He sees me and hears me. I may speak to Him. I will do my very best to please Him." With a good will, you can pray well — and God looks at your good will, knowing how weak you are.

St. Cyprian wrote, "When we stand praying . . . we ought to be watchful and earnest with our whole heart, intent on our prayers. Let all carnal and worldly thoughts pass away, and do not let the soul at that time think of anything except the object of its prayer."

To cultivate recollection implies that you willingly admit into your consciousness nothing that is inconsistent with the peaceful worship of God, except what duty demands. In the case of duty, what is admitted into your consciousness may disturb you for the moment, but it cannot really hurt you, so long as you hold fast to the will of God.

Remember St. Paul's principle: "To those who love God all things work together unto good!"[165] Try to secure the conditions that seem most favorable to your prayer; and if you cannot succeed in this, begin to pray to the best of your ability in the conditions that do exist, and leave the rest to God. Try to

[164] Ecclus. 18:23.
[165] Rom. 8:28.

avoid activities that, of their very nature, are contrary to the spirit of recollection.

∞

Try to keep your mind on your prayers

Do not disturb yourself about the distractions you may happen to have, but remain faithful, and lead your mind back gently to the subject that should be occupying you. At such a time, a book will help. All this presupposes that you try to lead a life of recollection by avoiding all distractions not imposed by the duties of your state of life and of charity.

You need not take a very deep interest in worldly affairs for which you are not responsible. Rather, take a lively interest in whatever has to do with God's honor and the good of your soul. Strive to become more like Jesus and aid Him in the salvation of souls. If you have little or no regard for these things, you will never learn to pray well, and you will be at least indirectly responsible for all the distractions that arise from these sometimes uncontrolled inclinations of your nature. This outward and inward detachment is so necessary for prayer because it is the Holy Spirit who prays in you. Since His action in your soul is very delicate, never oppose it. St. Paul says, "Do not grieve the Holy Spirit of God."[166] Yield yourself to Him, and put away everything that might oppose the freedom of the workings of His grace in your soul.

---

[166] Eph. 4:30 (RSV).

Part Four

∞

Perfect your prayer

Chapter Seventeen

ひ

Pray from your heart

Prayer is one of the chief duties of religion, and yet it does not come easily to us. A conscious effort is needed to gain union with God in prayer; free will must be exercised. You have surely had the experience that prayer is by no means easy; at times it entails a struggle against your natural inclinations. At times it is easy because you happen to be in the mood for it and God seems to be very near. Such feelings count for little in spiritual matters, since they are beyond your control and not subject to your will. God values the effort you make to gain union with Him in spite of natural difficulties.

In essence, love of God is not at all a matter of emotions or feelings, but, rather, it concerns the will. Feelings represent merely the satisfaction that you get out of love, and if a strong will is not ready to follow them up, they are next to useless. In fact, your love of God is never purer than when your soul keeps on blindly serving and seeking Him while experiencing no satisfaction whatsoever. The love of God consists in that supreme and sustained act of the will whereby you direct your whole heart and your whole mind to Him alone. Therefore, dryness in prayer should not disturb you.

∞

Learn to deal with dryness in prayer

Prayer is difficult for us because it is supernatural — that is, beyond the power of nature. When we pray, we lift ourselves from the natural into the supernatural, and for this we need the help of God. One of the great difficulties in prayer arises out of this strenuous effort to live in the supernatural order, which is strange to us. We are inclined to slip back to the natural. This is the reason for dryness and distractions in prayer. These suggestions may be helpful in times of dryness:

• *Prayer can be wordless.* Putting your sentiments into words, although often helpful, is not essential to communing with God. You can at times pray well without saying anything. Among people, the most welcome message of affection, understanding, or sympathy is often wordless. To friends, a grasp of the hand, a touch, a glance, or a smile may say more than speech could express. To God, the wordless movement of your will, unspoken self-surrender, loyalty, and trust, may perfectly fulfill the conditions of prayer.

Love's favorite language is silence. At Cana, our Lady said only, "They have no wine."[167] Her heart was sympathetic and grateful as she watched the waiters filling the waterpots with water. Magdalene silently anointed the feet of Jesus while her heart was filled with contrition.[168] The poor woman who was ill prayed confidently in her soul as she thought within herself, "If I but touch the

[167] John 2:3.
[168] Cf. John 12:3.

hem of His garment, I shall be healed."[169] Prayer in silence was implied when Jesus said, "Not everyone who says to me, 'Lord, Lord' shall enter the kingdom of Heaven, but he who does the will of my Father who is in Heaven."[170]

• *Use silent prayer while gazing thoughtfully upon a picture or statue* of our Lord or the Blessed Mother, or upon a picture depicting a religious scene, such as the Crucifixion. As sentiments of love, contrition, adoration, resignation, and admiration fill your soul — although you speak not a word — you are praying.

• *Take up a prayer book* and read a prayer that you like — slowly, thoughtfully, sincerely.

• *Have a childlike abandonment to God's loving Providence* in times of aridity in prayer and during the many distractions that may worry you when you are trying to pray. You should want not consolations, but the glory of God. As long as you are dissatisfied with yourself and try always to be better, all will be well. To be satisfied with your state may be a sign of pride or carelessness in the spiritual life. Try to be content with the wilderness through which the divine Shepherd is pleased to lead you, and do not stray off on your own to search for more pleasant pastures. The words of St. Teresa of Avila are consoling: "All that should be sought for in the exercise of prayer is conformity of our will with the divine will,

[169] Matt. 9:21.
[170] Matt. 7:21 (RSV).

in which consists the highest perfection." And John Henry Cardinal Newman states: "He who gives up regularity in prayer has lost a principal means of reminding himself that spiritual life is obedience to a Lawgiver, not a mere feeling or taste."

Prayer, then, requires no special feeling of devotion. Consolation in prayer is a secondary matter. If God gives you sweetness in prayer, be grateful for it. You can pray more easily with such help, but you can also pray without it.

∞

Learn to deal with distractions

Not all the distractions imaginable can keep you from pleasing God, if you refuse to entertain them. They make prayer more difficult, but they cannot make it fruitless. To persist in trying to lift up your mind and will to God is already to have succeeded in pleasing God. Here the intention counts.

The following advice on distractions at prayer may be helpful:

• *Try to be reverent during prayer*, keeping your eyes from wandering and keeping your body in proper position. Remember the dignity of God, with whom you converse. Prayer is an audience with God. A respectful attitude in the presence of God will help you to be attentive and earnest, whereas a careless attitude will distract you.

Outward reverence is a sign of a humble mind and, therefore, pleases God as much as humility itself does; and in His pleasure, He will hear you and give you His grace. It is not necessary to assume an uncomfortable position, but neither should you make yourself too comfortable at prayer. A slight mortification is helpful. Fix your eyes either on the altar or on some inspiring picture or statue, or keep them closed.

• *Repel distractions firmly but calmly* as soon as you become conscious of them. Do not be worried about the annoyance caused by distractions. Try to employ self-discipline and practical wisdom. Perhaps the most effective way of keeping an undesirable object out of your mind is to introduce another more interesting one. Focus your attention as long as possible on this and related subjects that follow one another into your mind. Thus, when undesirable images crowd in upon you at the time of prayer, you can fall back upon something rich, familiar, and interesting — for instance, a Gospel account, the incidents in the life of a saint, the mysteries of the Rosary, or the Stations of the Cross. The more you dwell on these, the more will you be able to rely on them. Each will become a cure for distractions in the degree that it has been assimilated.

Most distractions are bound up with the work you do. You may begin your prayer with the best of intentions only to find that you are thinking of your family, your business, your problems, your pleasures, or other interests. This is disturbing, but not sinful. You cannot leave such things outside as you can an overcoat or a hat. Your daily interests are always with you. They creep into your prayers without any conscious act on your part. Not until you become aware of them and then deliberately pursue them do you have a willful and therefore sinful distraction in prayer.

The only thing that will ruin vocal prayer is a really voluntary distraction, which turns your attention away from prayer and fixes it on something else that is not prayer, such as work or study.

Mental prayer requires a higher degree of attention than vocal prayer. Even involuntary distractions interrupt mental prayer. But the advantages of mental prayer, even interrupted by distractions, are so great that you should keep trying to develop it, even when it might seem too difficult for you. Do not be disturbed if the bustle of your daily life gets into your prayer. God knows that you are having difficulties and that you must fight hard to repel distractions. He will surely reward you for your persevering in this struggle.

Even the greatest saints have not been spared these tests of patience. They persisted loyally in their efforts to lift mind and will to God. St. Teresa of Avila said she could not even recite the Our Father without having to fight distractions. She had this to say about distractions: "There is something more which often afflicts those who practice the holy exercise of prayer. It is distractions. Distractions sometimes arise from unmortified senses, sometimes because the soul cannot for any length of time occupy itself with the same object; but often it is permitted by God to try His servant. What is to be done when one is distracted? We must suffer this humiliation with humility and patience. The time employed thus will not be lost. Such a prayer is oftentimes more advantageous than many made with recollection and sweetness, because, in banishing or supporting these distractions with the intention of pleasing God, we perform so many acts of love of God."

St. Brigid[171] suffered much in this way, and our Lady once appeared to her and said, "The Devil is wont to torment anyone who prays and to send him as many distractions as he can. But be not troubled on that account, my daughter, for although you may suffer from distractions, you can always have an earnest desire to pray well, and then your prayer will be pleasing to my Son."

The value of your prayer is not impaired by unnoticed and involuntary distractions, even though they may last a long time. It is more meritorious to fight distractions while praying than to enjoy bliss and consolation in your union with God.

• Never repeat a prayer because you want to make up for a distraction you may have had. The prayer you repeat is seldom better than it was the first time, and it may lead to scrupulosity. Repetition is unreasonable, for if the distraction came without your fault, it did not lessen the value of your prayer. If the distraction was your fault, it is far better to make up for your failing by an act of contrition. Humility must supply for the defects of all other virtues. At the close of a long prayer badly said, repeat, "O God, be merciful to me, a sinner" or "My Jesus, mercy!" and don't worry about it. If these words merited

---

[171] Possibly St. Brigid of Sweden (c. 1303-1373), founder of the Brigittines. — ED.

pardon for the publican,[172] why should they not obtain pardon for you?

• *Compose your own prayers.* The habit of doing so will help to fix your attention when your mind begins to wander. After all, only one thing remains essential: that you keep on praying. "He that shall persevere unto the end, he shall be saved."[173]

Suppose a good, kind father has four children. Three are bright, quick, and keen; the fourth is dull and simple. They go on a picnic. When they return, they all have much to relate. The three bright ones tell their story of the day's adventures in a pleasant, interesting way. The simple child speaks hazily and disconnectedly. He wanders from subject to subject. Will the father be angry and turn away from the afflicted child in disgust? No, rather, his fatherly sympathy will have pity on the child and encourage him.

God is a kind Father. We are all His more or less dull and simple children when compared with the angels, who never wander in their adoration and praise of Him.

Since we cannot avoid involuntary distractions in prayer, let us turn them into a source of merit, by bearing them humbly and patiently. Discouragement easily follows such efforts at attention in prayer. You must guard against discouragement and be patient with your nature. You must persevere in spite of difficulty in the effort to keep in touch with God. Once you

[172] Cf. Luke 18:9-14.
[173] Matt. 10:22.

are discouraged, the Devil finds it easy to persuade you to give up the effort of prayer. You must go on trying in the face of this difficulty to keep in touch with God. With His help, you will persevere.

∞

Make your prayer personal

Perhaps you make prayer more difficult because you do not talk to God as friend to friend. Let there be nothing unnatural in the words you use, nothing impersonal in the sense that you try to be something you are not.

Prayer must be personal and express what you really mean to say. You must pray in the method that suits you. It must be your prayer, not someone else's.

A prayer poured out in your own words has the best chance of being personal, sincere, and real. You do not quote passages from books to make conversation with a dear friend, although bookish expressions would be more graceful. Sincerity is the essential element of prayer. So do not be afraid to speak to God in your own words, as a child speaks to a father, as a friend converses with the best of friends.

A prayer book is merely a model, not *your* prayer. If the poetic or formal language you find in some prayers does not appeal to you, do not use them, or they will become unnatural and burdensome. How simple the publican's prayer: "O God, be merciful to me, a sinner!"[174] Talk with God in your own words as much as possible. He knows you better than any friend. Be yourself. Although ready-made prayers may help,

[174] Luke 18:13.

they do not fit all. Be honest enough not to say what you do not mean.

Avoid reciting prayers so fast as to make praying not only impersonal but irreverent. You will find value in praying with extraordinary slowness, dwelling on each word as long as you find appropriate meaning, consolation, and strength in considering it. Sometimes a single word, such as the word *Father*, possesses a wonderful power to arouse deep feeling. You may repeat the word as your soul reaches out toward God to adore Him, to thank Him, to love Him, or to submit to His will, or your mind may pause to look at the word from many angles and admire its hidden meanings.

God is pleased by simple, heartfelt, personal expressions of love as we turn to Him in prayer.

⚭

Make frequent use of short prayers

If you find prayer very irksome, do not try to pray for a long time. Speak to God as a friend as long as you wish; then keep silent. In prayer, some people are inclined to do all the talking and do not give God the opportunity to speak to them. God speaks to you in the silence of your heart. Perhaps you give Him little chance to speak.

God does not want you to read to Him at length out of a book. He wants to hear all about your interests and needs, to share your personal life. He does not expect you to be talking all the time. Friends can be quite happy together in silence. In the Sermon on the Mount, our Lord said, "In praying, do not heap up empty phrases as the Gentiles do; for they think they will be heard for their many words. Do not be like them, for your Father knows what you need before you ask Him."[175] He then gave us that beautiful prayer, the Our Father, in plain, simple, yet deep and meaningful words.

St. Benedict,[176] who lived in the sixth century, wrote in his rule, "Let us be sure that we shall not be heard for our much speaking, but for purity of heart and tears of compunction. Our prayer, therefore, ought to be short and pure, unless it chance to be prolonged by the impulse and inspiration of divine grace."

Perhaps you can more easily keep in touch with God by means of frequent aspirations — that is, brief, spontaneous prayers — throughout the day, rather than by trying to spend some time in praying and then, thinking your duty done, forget about God. Just as the thought of a friend will often come to your mind, so if you really look on God as a friend, you cannot help thinking of Him at times during the day, asking for mercy, begging a favor, and praising His goodness.

The very thought of God can be a prayer. It does not require deep spirituality to raise your mind to the thought of God and so to pray to Him. The more you accustom yourself to this frequent thought of God, the more will you be able to live with God in your heart, and the more you will pray and increase in His grace.

Since conversation with God need not be conducted in polished phrases, aspirations have a special excellence in our prayer life. Many of the saints made their prayers short and frequent rather than long. Imagine St. Peter saying, "Christ, Son

---

[175] Matt. 6:7-8 (RSV).

[176] St. Benedict (c. 480-c. 550), Father of Western monasticism.

of the living God";[177] St. Thomas saying, "My Lord and my God";[178] St. Mary Magdalene saying, "Rabboni";[179] St. John saying, "The Word was made flesh";[180] and St. Thérèse saying, "O my God, I love Thee." It should not be difficult to make these and similar phrases your own, and to repeat them many times a day, each new utterance arousing a new movement of your soul toward God and a deepening of your love for Him.

Try to find some method of prayer to suit your temperament and keep you in close touch with God. Prayer is union with God; no matter how you attain this union, prayer is doing its work in your soul.

[177] Matt. 16:16.
[178] John 20:28.
[179] John 20:16.
[180] John 1:14.

Chapter Eighteen

Overcome the obstacles to prayer

If prayer has not produced in your soul in greater measure some of its wonderful effects, it is because you permit obstacles to remain in the way of your union with God. These obstacles come under the headings of pride, selfishness, and sin. Such obstacles weaken and even destroy the spirit of prayer.

∞

Try to be detached from creatures

There are degrees of love. The lowest degree is to love God, while you love other good things as well and for their own sakes. The highest degree is to love God alone with all your power, and people and things just because of Him and in Him.

You should not become so attached to temporal goods as to allow them to cause you to forget God by carelessness in your duty to pray. If your heart is full of the desires for worldly things, God has little or no room there.

You are truly detached from creatures only in the measure that you are attached to God and you love all creatures in the Creator and the Creator in all creatures. Detachment is not, therefore, a cold-hearted indifference to beauty and the joys of

God's creation. If you really love God, you are in a position to appreciate and use to the best advantage the creatures of this earth. Even in friendship, you can love God in the person who is your friend. You lack harmony in your spiritual life when you concentrate so exclusively on what you consider purely spiritual things that you neglect the material expressions of the spirit. All the creatures of God are good, and although you deny yourself them, you do this not because they are not good, but for the sake of a greater good that comprises all lesser good. You should be able to use with high appreciation all the gifts of God at one time or another and when they are not incompatible with your state of life.

But the hustle and bustle of your own workaday life may be a source of much distraction to you. You may even use this as an excuse not to pray. Under such circumstances, you need to unite yourself with God in prayer even more, lest you become estranged from God.

St. Jerome[181] has some good advice for the busy parent: "Moderate sufficiently the solicitude which animates you in the care of your house, that you may still have a few moments left over to employ for the spiritual necessities of your soul. Seek a proper place sufficiently removed from the noise of your family, where you call shelter yourself against the tempest occasioned by the multitude of your occupations and where you may in the silence of solitude appease the turbulent flood of your thoughts. . . . Let your zeal for divine reading be so great, your prayers so frequent, your thought of the future life so constant, as to balance the occupations of the rest of your

---

[181] St. Jerome (c. 342-420), biblical scholar.

time. We say this not to take you away from your family, but with the idea that there you will learn and meditate on how to act with them."

St. Ignatius offers good advice to the busy working person: "Remember always to make many withdrawals into the solitude of your heart while you are outwardly taken up with business; and this mental solitude cannot be hindered by the multitude of those who are around you, but only around your body, so that your heart may remain all alone in the presence of God."

Recollection, therefore, is very important in order to foster the spirit of prayer. Blessed Henry Suso[182] wrote, "If you would desire that union with God which seeks to please Him alone in all things, do not lose sight of recollection in your manner of life and in conversation. Live as much as possible within your interior; think of God, who dwells there; hasten to banish from your heart all that you have heard or seen from without. Your heart will be dilated; you will run in the way of His commandments; you will make it your delight to do His will."

You cannot pray if creatures occupy your imagination, your mind, and especially your heart, and at the same time exclude God. Purity of soul, very necessary as a preparation for prayer, deepens your love for God.

∽

Be ready to do all that pleases God

A spirit of self-denial is necessary if there is to be depth in prayer. You cannot expect to reach intimacy with God by prayer if you are continually reaching out for the pleasures of

---

[182] Blessed Henry Suso (c. 1295-1366), German mystic.

the world. You must be ready to sacrifice much that is merely pleasurable without being sinful. St. Thomas More,[183] who was martyred for the Faith in England in the sixteenth century, wrote, "Not only pleasure will withdraw men from prayer, but also affliction sometimes; but there is this difference: affliction will sometimes extort a short prayer from the wickedest man alive, but pleasure stifles it altogether."

Christ never allows Himself to be outdone in generosity. When you are ready to sacrifice yourself for Him, a new joy comes into your life to which no earthly joy can be compared.

Your heart must be purified before it can live the life of intimate prayer and union with God. Christ is the way to the Father, for He said, "I am the way, and the truth, and the life. . . . No man comes to the Father but by me."[184] Your task, then, is to come into the closest possible contact with the Heart of Jesus. Sin and selfishness in varied forms stand in the way of this contact with Him. Jesus does not delight in seeing you suffer. It is not sacrifice in itself that is of any great value. In fact, sacrifice is simply pain unless there is love in it. You must be willing to give up whatever may stand between you and the love of Christ. The divine life can flow into your soul only in the measure in which your soul is emptied of selfishness and sin. And this demands self-sacrifice. Jesus said that the grain of wheat must die in order to bring forth much fruit.[185] Pride, selfishness, and sin must be conquered before Christ can reign supreme.

---

[183] St. Thomas More (1478-1535), Lord Chancellor of England.
[184] John 14:6.
[185] John 12:24.

Therefore, refuse nothing that God may ask of you. Yield your soul to God by fulfilling His divine will after the example of Christ, who said, "I do always the things that please Him."[186]

Be generous when the Holy Spirit shows you some failing that you should correct, or some sacrifice you should make, or some good you should do. Love for God will lead you to do all you can to please God and refuse Him nothing.

A lack of generosity is expressed by complaining when things grow difficult to bear. We blame God for evil instead of praying to God to be delivered from it.

∞

Trust in God's Providence

An ancient manuscript, whose author is unknown, says, "The highest perfection of a pure and sincere life depends upon this: Man must, out of true love for God, willingly and fully commit himself to His Providence and, without exception, subject his own will to the divine, frequently and often. Also, with a deep and burning desire, he must constantly elevate his heart to God and repeat the words 'My loving God and Father, when will I love You with all my heart and all my soul and all my mind, as You commanded me? When will I, being wretchedly dependent, fulfill Your divine will, be wholly subjected to it, and think, speak and desire nothing but what pleases Your divine Majesty? May Your holy name be honored and Your glory be sung now and in all eternity.' What grace and true interior joy and peace will be the portion of him who is filled with such desires and who practices such complete subjection of spirit to

---

[186] John 8:29.

God, no one can know, much less declare, except him who has experienced it."

The care which God has over His earthly children was beautifully explained by our Lord when He said, "And as for clothing, why are you anxious? Consider how the lilies of the field grow; they neither toil nor spin, yet I say to you that not even Solomon in all his glory was arrayed like one of these. But if God so clothes the grass of the field, which today is alive and tomorrow is thrown into the oven, how much more you, O you of little faith! Therefore do not be anxious, saying, 'What shall we eat?' or, 'What shall we drink?' or, 'What are we to put on?' (for after all these things the Gentiles seek); for your heavenly Father knows that you need all these things. But seek first the kingdom of God and His justice, and all these things shall be yours as well."[187]

Few things are more detrimental to the spirit of prayer than worry. God will most certainly not fail you if you are generous with Him, and cast yourself and your cares upon Him, seeking nothing but His glory. Of course, you must take every reasonable precaution, and then you can leave the issue in God's hands with perfect confidence. The issue may not be what you might have hoped for, but it will be for your eternal good. If you really seek God, there is no event in your life that will not further your progress toward Him.

Many good persons are under the impression that if they were living almost anywhere but where they happen to be at the moment, they would be able to serve God much better than they do. This frame of mind indicates a large degree of

[187] Matt. 6:28-33 (RSV).

self-seeking: you want peace and recollection for yourself. If you really seek God and seek nothing for yourself, you will find peace and recollection wherever the Providence of God has arranged for you to be. Learn to serve God not as you want, but as He wants. You will do this by serving Him in the circumstances in which you are placed.

A childlike abandonment to the loving Providence of God is absolutely necessary, lest you worry without reason and thereby disturb your union with God in prayer. You may make mistakes, but the mistakes you make with the pure intention of seeking God will be turned by His divine power to your advantage and His glory.

Trusting in God's Providence will help you to carry the load of your faults and sins with deep sorrow and a firm purpose of amendment, without surprise and without discouragement. You acknowledge that you are a sinner, but you know that what really matters is what you want to be and what you earnestly are trying to be.

You have only the present moment to offer to God. You may be so busy thinking of what you shall do next that you miss the opportunities that lie before you — and opportunities do not come again. Remember St. Augustine's advice: "Leave the past to God's mercy, the future to His Divine Providence, and the present to His love."

◌◌

Love of neighbor is essential to prayer

We must be at peace with our neighbor if we expect God to grant our prayer. We cannot love God as we ought without at the same time loving our neighbor. Love of our neighbor is a proof of our love of God, because we love our neighbor for the love of God.

If you harbor bitterness and a spirit of unforgiveness in your heart, you are putting an obstacle in the way of your prayer. How can you expect God to be generous with you when you refuse to be generous with your neighbor, who is a creature and a child of God? God will not listen to your prayer if your heart is poisoned with bitterness against another.

Our Lord said, "If thou art offering thy gift at the altar, and there rememberest that thy brother has anything against thee, leave thy gift before the altar and go first to be reconciled to thy brother, and then come and offer thy gift."[188]

Our Lord also said, "When you stand up to pray, forgive whatever you have against anyone, so that your Father in Heaven may also forgive you your offenses."[189] God will hardly listen to a prayer coming from an unkind and unforgiving heart. The neglect of the greatest of all commandments — which is the fulfillment of the whole law — cannot be supplied by any other good work.

God is moved by the effort you make to forgive your neighbor and to cleanse your heart of all bitterness, even though you may consider it justifiable. There can be no peace with God in prayer if there is no peace with your neighbor. A spirit of forgiveness merits God's forgiveness of your own sins, and the peace that accompanies it.

[188] Matt. 5:23-24.
[189] Mark 11:25.

Chapter Nineteen

∞

Make a good intention to please God

Our Lord said that we "must pray always and not lose heart."[190]
St. Paul teaches the same doctrine both by word and example:
"Rejoice always, pray constantly, give thanks in all circumstances, for this is the will of God in Christ Jesus for you."[191]

But how can you pray without ceasing and still carry out
your daily duties? Two things are required:

+ *Say those prayers faithfully which are required by your
state in life:* morning and night prayers, meal prayers,
private and family rosary; prayers said at least at an occasional weekday Mass, at weekly — if not daily — Holy
Communion, at visits to the Blessed Sacrament, evening devotions and Benediction, the Stations of the
Cross, and so on.

+ *Turn your ordinary actions into prayer.* The subject of
prayers required by your state of life has been treated.
The question now is: How can you turn your ordinary

[190] Luke 18:1.
[191] 1 Thess. 5:16-18 (RSV).

actions into prayer? You can do so by making a good intention and by walking in the presence of God.

∽

Do all for the glory of God

God made us to show forth His goodness and to share with us His everlasting happiness in Heaven. And what must we do to gain the happiness of Heaven? We must know, love, and serve God in this world.

St. Paul expresses this truth briefly: "Do all for the glory of God."[192] It is our duty and mission here below to honor God as our Lord and Creator, as our goal and last end.

You were created for eternal happiness with God in Heaven. Everything else must take second place in your life, because if you lose Heaven, you lose everything. The sure guide to Heaven is God's holy will. If you follow it in your daily life, your every action on earth will be a step in the direction of God and the perfect happiness that your heart craves.

God expresses His will in His commandments. His great commandment is: "Thou shalt love the Lord thy God with thy whole heart, and with thy whole soul, and with thy whole mind." And the second is like it: "Thou shalt love thy neighbor as thyself."[193] The love of God and of neighbor is both the summary and the fullness of the law.

Jesus said, "If you love me, keep my commandments."[194] And again, "If you keep my commandments, you will abide in

---

[192] Cf. 1 Cor. 10:31.
[193] Matt. 22:37, 39.
[194] John 14:15.

my love, as I also have kept my Father's commandments and abide in His love."[195]

Thus the law of charity commands you to love God with your whole heart. To do this, you must put everything in proper relationship to Him. You cannot fulfill the commandment of charity unless you relate everything you do to God. To relate an act to God means to perform it with a good intention.

Therefore, to have a good intention means to perform your actions in order to please God and to do His will, and thereby gain Heaven. It is God's will that you do all things out of love for Him. Love directs your whole life toward God. The practical means of giving all your actions this direction is to offer each of them out of love to the Most Blessed Trinity in union with Jesus Christ and in accordance with His intentions.

The whole of the spiritual life may be described as the quest of the soul for God alone. True holiness seeks God alone, and it is the fruit of the love of God. Perfection is the result of perfect love, of perfectly fulfilling the catechism precept to know, love, and serve God. Although this is within the scope of all, it calls for courage and generosity. Love of God lifts the monotonous routine of your life out of the ordinary to a level in which your love for God becomes the inspiration of your least action and God's love for you becomes the source of all the events and circumstances of your life. Whatever happens, whatever joys or sorrows come your way, you must always keep your will firmly fixed on God alone. Then, no matter what temptations may assail you, even if you fall but rise again, you will surely reach the goal.

[195] John 15:10.

⁂

Have a good intention in all things

God wants you to have a supernatural purpose in whatever you do, think, or say. Whether you are trying to avoid Hell, shorten your Purgatory, or gain merit for Heaven, such motives are supernatural, and therefore they are good intentions. Sometimes you are unaware of your motives, but as long as you are not in mortal sin, and your action agrees with God's commandments, you have a good intention.

But a good intention may have different degrees of perfection. Thus, when you do something out of love for God, to please Him, your intention is higher than if you think of your own advantage.

On the other hand, to act with a bad intention means to intend something that runs counter to the commandments of God and the Church. A bad intention comes from the evil desires of the eyes, of the flesh, or pride of life.[196] Whatever you do from such motives can never please God or aid in your salvation.

God might speak to you in this way: "I am your highest goal. You cannot be happy in tending toward any other. Those who serve me willingly and faithfully receive many graces. But those who glory in self or in anything else but me will not find true peace and joy; rather, they will find many obstacles in their way."

Our good deeds merit Heaven, but our deeds are not really good and meritorious if they are done with selfish or evil motives.

[196] Cf. 1 John 2:16.

∞

A good intention renders your
works good in the eyes of God

Our Lord says, "The lamp of the body is the eye. If thy eye is sound, thy whole body will be full of light. But if thy eye is evil, thy whole body will be full of darkness."[197] The eye of the soul is the intention, which is sound when the soul is turned toward God in all that it does; but when it is turned away from God and looks at something else, the eye is evil, and the work is dark.

St. Augustine says, "The good intention is, as it were, the soul of a good work. As the body without the soul is dead, so a work is dead in the eyes of God if it is not performed with a good intention." And St. Francis de Sales wrote, "Little actions are great when they are done well. A little action done for the glory of God, with a great desire to please Him, is more agreeable to Him than a great one performed with less fervor. We must, then, strive especially to do little things well which are so easy, and which offer themselves at every moment, if we would grow in the friendship of God. . . . To do our actions well, we must perform them with a very pure intention and a very decided and joyous will to please God alone. This is the body, the soul, of our actions; it is this that gives them their value, that makes them easy and agreeable."

The purer your good intention is, the greater is the worth of the works you perform. By means of it, your smallest deeds become great and important in God's sight. This explains the praise that Jesus gave to the poor widow who offered her mite

[197] Matt. 6:22-23.

in the temple. "And Jesus, sitting over against the treasury, and beheld how the people cast money into the treasury; and many that were rich cast in much. And came a certain poor widow, and she cast in two mites. . . . And calling His disciples together, He saith to them, 'Amen, I say to you, this poor widow hath cast in more than they who have cast into the treasury. For all they have cast in of their abundance; but she of her want cast in all she had, even her whole living.' "[198]

Jesus pointed to the poor widow and made known her good deed, with all the circumstances that made it so precious in God's eyes. Filled with deep religious earnestness, she was determined to fulfill all the duties of religion at any cost and under all circumstances, without regard for self. In a spirit of generosity, she trusted in God's Providence, not looking at what she was bound to do, but at what she could do. She did her utmost with great reverence and love for God and did not esteem her own action.

Through her example, Jesus teaches you that it is not what you do for God, but the love with which you do it that makes your actions pleasing to Him, and that even the smallest act of love is precious in His eyes. In the praise He gave the poor widow, He stressed the value of a good intention. The widow performed her generous deed in order to please God and to do His will. Her action was prompted by love, and it was this love that made her gift, small as it was, very precious in God's sight.

Our Lord does not measure our perfection by the number and greatness of the works we do, but by the manner in which

[198] Mark 12:41-44.

we do them, and this manner is the love with which they are performed, becoming more pure and more perfect. This is why St. John of the Cross[199] could say, "The least movement of pure love is of more value to the Church than all other works united together." And St. Thérèse, who studied the spirit of St. John of the Cross, said, "Without love, our works, even the most brilliant, count as nothing. Jesus does not demand from us great deeds, but only gratitude and self-surrender; that is to say, love."

By making a good intention, you will convert all of your actions, even your recreation and repose, into a hymn of praise to God's glory. St. Paul wrote, "Whatever you do in word or in work, do all in the name of the Lord Jesus Christ, giving thanks to God the Father through Him."[200]

∞

A good intention gives enduring worth to your life

You live on earth but once, so you must endeavor to profit from everything that happens to you. In the end, nothing will remain with you except God, your good works, and eternity. So invest all your ability and time for eternity; it will be a good investment.

No one can be as grateful to you as God for the least service you take upon yourself for the love of Him. Make the good intention govern your whole conduct. All actions not animated

---

[199] St. John of the Cross (1542-1591), mystical Doctor and joint founder of the Discalced Carmelites.
[200] Col. 3:17.

by the desire to do God's will are like rivulets that sooner or later disappear in the sand without leaving a trace. But that which is done for God remains and becomes a mighty stream emptying into the ocean of a blessed eternity.

Our Lord speaks of a right intention in these words: "Do not lay up for yourselves treasures on earth, where rust and moth consume, and where thieves break in and steal; but lay up for yourselves treasures in Heaven, where neither rust nor moth consumes, nor thieves break in and steal. For where thy treasure is, there your heart also will be."[201] Do not lay up treasures on earth, but in Heaven. A heavenly reward — the possession of God — will last forever. God is your treasure; let your heart be centered upon Him by living a life of love, doing all, suffering all, for the love of God. Such a life means "praying always."

∞

Learn how to make a good intention

The following suggestions will help you to make a good intention:

• *Briefly recall to mind that God is in your soul,* that He sees you and earnestly desires that you consecrate to Him whatever you do or suffer, and then say a short prayer of love offering your action to God. You may use aspirations of love such as these:

All for You,
most Sacred Heart of Jesus!

[201] Matt. 6:19-21 (RSV).

Make a good intention to please God

Sacred Heart of Jesus,
I give myself to You
through Mary!

Sweet Heart of Jesus,
be my love!

Most Holy Trinity,
dwelling in my soul by Your grace,
make me love You more and more!

Jesus, for love of You,
with You and for You!

Jesus, my God,
I love You above all things!

Mary, make me live in God,
with God, and for God!

Make your good intention each morning in your
morning prayers by using a form such as this:

O Jesus, through the Immaculate Heart of Mary,
I offer Thee my prayers, works, joys, and sufferings
of this day for all the intentions of Thy Sacred Heart,
in union with the Holy Sacrifice of the Mass
throughout the world, in reparation for my sins,
for the intentions of all our associates, and in
particular for all the intentions of the Holy Father.

• *Renew your good intention frequently,* as the clock strikes
the hour or at a pause in your work, or whenever you
have a spare moment. Your intention tends to become

dim as you go through your daily occupations. Gradually you are influenced more and more by pleasure or self-satisfaction. Therefore, renew your pure intention at different times during the day.

St. Francis de Sales offers this advice: "Think of God during the time that you are occupied. If He abandons you, you cannot make a step without falling. Imitate little children, who, with one hand, cling to their mother, while they do as they will with the other. In all your actions turn yourself from time to time toward your heavenly Father, to see if that which you do is pleasing to Him, and to implore help. You will do better what you have to do, and you will find that easy which before was difficult. Represent to yourself Mary, using one hand to work while with the other she holds the divine Infant."

While it is not necessary to make a good intention before every action that you perform, it is necessary, as St. Thomas Aquinas says, to have the general intention of doing everything for the glory of God. St. Thomas himself would often write the words "*Ave, Maria*" or "O God, I love You" in the middle of the sentences of his manuscript. Even as he worked, he loved God and His Blessed Mother.

• *Do not make a distinction between agreeable and disagreeable occupations.* Regardless of feelings, moods, prejudices, or preferences, strive to maintain a good intention at all times. Be just as ready to feel suffering as to feel joy; be just as glad to be poor as to be well off. Follow God's will in all things. As soon as your natural desires contradict God's will, check them as you would check any other foolish intention. If you prefer God's will in all things, you will be preferring the perfect wisdom and the highest good.

If you really want to please God, you will gladly apply yourself to every task imposed upon you because it is the will of God. You should consider it an honor to perform all your duties with equal devotion, without letting anyone know what you like and what you dislike. Where the glory of God is involved, there is nothing that you should not be willing to do. The saints did everything for the love of God, whether the actions were pleasant or unpleasant.

God made and controls all things in your daily life. How can you forget this truth and complain about anything? Try to be equally willing to receive from His hand the sweet and the bitter, the joy and the sorrow. Thank Him for whatever He decides to send you. Only keep away from sin, and you will fear neither death nor Hell. Whatever suffering comes to you will not hurt you for long. Ask God for the grace to see, love, and prefer His will in everything that happens to you.

• *Do not pay too much attention to the outward success of your work,* nor to the recognition which it receives or does not receive from others. If you are in earnest about pleasing God, you will not trouble yourself very much about anything else. Too many are disturbed about the way people regard their actions, which makes little or no difference as long as the action is pleasing to God.

Do not let life's daily failures or disappointments disturb or affect you too much. God made you for the perfect life of Heaven. Whatever He sends you is sent with this goal in view. Some things you can remedy and improve in your daily life, whereas other things are beyond your control. After you have done your best, you should accept the results as God's will for you. Be it hard or easy, pleasant or disagreeable, you can always be sure that God knows, wants, and permits what is good for your soul. Try to know God's will and to accept it in all things. With this pure intention, you will have a deep interior peace, God's gift to those who let Him govern their lives.

Complaining about lack of success and recognition shows that you are not seeking God and Heaven with a pure intention.

Do all things to please God, and do not be discouraged if people fail to recognize the good you do or think or say. God sees and understands, and that is all that matters, for He will reward you. Do not be too eager to have your work recognized. Your praise should consist in pleasing God. You will never go wrong in measuring your success by the ever-increasing beauty of sanctifying grace in your soul and the degree of merit you are gaining for Heaven. If you have meant well and have done your best, you are sure of God's recognition and of eternal success, and that ought to fill your soul with so much peace and joy that you can cheerfully dispense with human praise.

If you have performed a good action or achieved some success, remember it was accomplished only with the help of God. Offer the deed to God, and then dispel the thought of it from your mind. People may not notice the good deed; even you may pass over it lightly, but God will not forget it. You cannot stop doing good; you must continue laying up for yourself treasures in Heaven until the day you die.

• *Do not seek pleasure purely for its own sake in things that gratify nature*, such as in eating, sleeping, and recreation. Yet even these things have value according to God's way of thinking. St. Paul says, "Whether you eat or drink, or whatsoever else you do, do all for the glory of God."[202] Even your pleasure should improve you in some way and make you better able to do your work. God wants you to live a sinless and useful life. The pleasures and joys that make you worse will make your death and judgment a little harder to face. If you truly love God, you will hate everything that holds you back from Him. He alone, the eternal, infinite good, the perfect joy of your soul, can bring true peace and unending happiness to your heart.

• *Rejoice when others achieve success and gain recognition no less than if you had done so yourself.* As long as God is glorified, nothing else matters! An unselfish spirit will certainly be rewarded by God. Kind thoughts lead you to do more good by allowing you to share in the good that others do. The noble acts of others may be yours in the sight of God, if, when you notice them, you offer

[202] 1 Cor. 10:31.

167

them with a prayer and good wishes. You cooperate in God's work when you wish your neighbor well, when you ask God's blessing on his work, and when you rejoice and thank God for his humble success.

• *Do not place your confidence in your own ability, but unite your intentions and labors with those of Jesus Christ and His Blessed Mother.* In this way, you will share in the merits of the Son of God and His Mother, and they will supply whatever may be lacking in your disposition and work.

In Jesus, you have power to know and to fulfill the holy will of God, whether it be to work for His honor or to suffer all things for His glory. Jesus is in you through His grace, in order to make you a partaker of His divine life and to make you and your actions holy. He wants to fill all the faculties of your soul with His own Self, to be the light of your mind by showing you what you must do and what you must avoid, and to be the strength of your will so that you may be able to do what is right. He said, "Without me, you can do nothing."[203]

Renounce your own wishes and feelings in order to enter into the wishes and feelings of Jesus Christ, and then you will give glory to God in the highest way, as St. Paul advised: "Let this mind be in you which was also in Christ Jesus."[204]

If you wish to live an interior life of prayer, let it be your pride and your pleasure to do, think, and act all for

[203] John 15:5.
[204] Phil. 2:5.

God. God should be constantly present to you. He should live in your consciousness, to the end that your will may be directed solely by one norm: All for God!

Firmly anchored in God, you will feel a sweet compulsion before every labor — and frequently during its course — to raise your heart and soul to God, who is your all. The praise of the world will leave you unmoved. Although grateful to the well-wisher, you will all the while recall in your innermost heart: Lord, You know all things, You know also that I love only You and, hence, that I have labored and suffered for You alone!

Chapter Twenty

∞

Walk in God's presence

Another means of turning your ordinary actions into prayer is the practice of walking in the presence of God. It consists in remembering the presence of God in order to make progress in holiness. You are not alone; God is with you. He accompanies you wherever you go. He observes you at work. He hears and judges whatever you say. He knows your most secret thoughts.

When you pray, you seek the God of light. Your soul enters into light. St. John, who soared in prayer like the eagle, high up into the blinding rays of the divinity, tells us, "God is light, and in Him there is no darkness."[205] St. Paul writes that God is He who dwells in light inaccessible.[206] To pray means to step out of the darkness of this earth, to separate yourself at least in thought and desire from the pressure of external things, and to bathe your soul in that ocean of light which is the divinity. The psalmist says, "The light of Thy countenance, O Lord, is signed upon us; Thou hast given gladness in my heart."[207]

[205] 1 John 1:5.
[206] 1 Tim. 6:16.
[207] Ps. 4:7 (RSV = Ps. 4:6-7).

This is why you should enter upon your prayer with much care and, especially at the beginning, with a conscious turning to the presence of God. The light of the presence of God floods the temple of your soul when you pray.

By nature, you have a strong tendency to make created things — and particularly yourself — the center of all of your thoughts and actions. This causes you to put the love and service of God into the background, in a more or less secondary place. This constant upsurge of earthly interests prevents your soul from being conscious of the presence of God. In such a state, the truths of Faith cannot influence your way of life. But none of your occupations should claim your attention so completely as not to allow you time to remember the presence of God.

The practice of walking in the presence of God is very valuable for your spiritual life, for it will produce a salutary effect on your soul. By degrees you will reach a point at which you always feel that you are not alone, but with and in God. Guided by the impulse of grace, you will acquire the good habit of frequently talking to God in your heart in acts of adoration, thanksgiving, contrition, and petition. You will declare your good intention of doing all things for the honor and glory of God. Walking in the presence of God will teach you to live a life of love in union with God, and this is genuine holiness.

Hence, all your actions will become like a prayer, for this practice applies to all your actions and renders them supernatural and holy. Along with the renewal of the good intention, it is one of the best ways of turning your actions into prayer and fulfilling the Savior's wish that you "pray always."

To walk in the presence of God, apply to yourself the following three revealed truths:

• *God is present everywhere.* He is present in every place, not only by His knowledge and power, but also by His essence and activity. Everything that exists is preserved and enabled to operate by Him. You would not exist were it not for Him. From Him you have life and strength; without Him you cannot move, see, speak, think, or will.

Walking in the presence of God makes you think of God and turn to Him in loving prayer when you see a beautiful flower, or majestic trees, or a placid lake, or a star-studded winter sky. God is very close to you in the things He made. Take time to notice His handiwork, and you will be drawn to love Him more. If His creatures are so wonderful, how wonderful must Infinite Goodness and Beauty be!

In the psalms, we read, "Whither shall I go from Thy spirit? Or whither shall I flee from Thy face? If I ascend into Heaven, Thou art there; if I descend into hell, Thou art present. If I take my wings early in the morning, and dwell in the uttermost parts of the sea, even there also shall Thy hand lead me, and Thy right hand shall hold me."[208]

• *Jesus is present in the Blessed Sacrament.* He is present in the Holy Eucharist with His body and blood, soul and divinity, with all the love of His heart and the

[208] Ps. 138:7-10 (RSV = Ps. 139:7-10).

whole treasury of His merits. He observes you as you go about your work; His thoughts and prayers are devoted to you; He never forgets you even for one moment, day or night. What a powerful influence His presence in the tabernacle can exert on your life if only you would remember that He is there for you! Your thoughts should turn to Him in loving prayers as you go about your daily tasks.

Daily Mass and Communion are occasions of most intimate union with Jesus. The act of Communion itself is passing, but the effect it produces — union with Christ by love — is meant to be permanent; it lasts as long as and in the measure that you wish. Jesus does not dwell with you bodily after the Sacred Species are consumed, yet He does dwell with you by the outpourings of His love, by the lights and graces He sends you from the tabernacle without ceasing. This is what He meant when He said the night before He died, "Abide in me, and I in you. As the branch cannot bear fruit of itself unless it remains on the vine, so neither can you unless you abide in me."[209] A very useful means of increasing and perfecting your union with Jesus throughout the day is by the repetition of acts of love. It is impossible for you to formulate continually definite acts of love. But you can, with God's grace, so multiply them that they dominate all your actions, exercise on your life a more penetrating influence, and change all your actions into a prayer.

[209] John 15:4.

It is easy to make an act of love. A simple movement of the heart is enough. In this manner, the humblest action and the least sacrifice can be transformed into an act of love. The smallest act of pure love has more value in God's eyes than all other acts united.

• *The Holy Spirit dwells in you.* The Third Person of the Blessed Trinity not only is present in your soul by His essence and power, but also loves you so dearly that He does not wish to be away from you. St. Paul wrote, "Do you not know that you are God's temple and that God's Spirit dwells in you?"[210]

The Holy Spirit proves His love for you by His wonderful activity in your soul. He clothes your soul with the glorious garment of sanctifying grace and adorns it with the infused virtues and His sevenfold gifts, thus enlightening and strengthening it, inciting it to good, and supporting and perfecting it in goodness. He has consecrated your soul as His temple and dwells there as your constant Guest. He watches over you, knows about all you do, and loves you with an infinite love, for He is the God of love.

As long as you are in the state of sanctifying grace, the Holy Spirit lives in your soul as in a temple. There He gives you all the graces you need to avoid sin and to practice virtue. Remember the Holy Spirit in your soul, and frequently turn to Him in loving prayer. The faithful attention to His dwelling and working within

[210] 1 Cor. 3:16 (RSV).

your soul will lead you to an ever-deepening understanding of this gracious gift of Himself. This blissful familiarity in which your soul enjoys His divine presence, and the readiness with which you listen to His inspirations, is the very heart of special veneration of the Holy Spirit.

Walking in the presence of God the Holy Spirit, dwelling in your soul, is a fulfillment of the earnest wish of our divine Savior, who said the night before He died, "I will ask the Father, and He will give you another Advocate to dwell with you forever, the Spirit of truth whom the world cannot receive, because it neither sees Him nor knows Him. But you shall know Him, because He will dwell with you and be in you."[211]

∞

Walking in God's presence
will help your prayer

To live an interior life of prayer means to walk in the presence of God; it demands a mind constantly anchored in God. Never to lose sight of God, never to leave His side, always to move in His presence — these are necessities, as well as joys, for the soul steeped in the interior life.

As far as it is in your power, try to keep in touch with God. Do not let yourself be diverted from this path of union with God. Whether alone or in company, at work or at recreation, do not allow your soul to leave His presence. Find ways and means to raise your heart to God.

[211] Cf. John 14:16-17.

Let God live in your heart. Let your first thought on arising, and your last thought at night, be of Him. Without effort, lead your thoughts back to God throughout the day, by a glance at a picture, by the striking of the hour, at work and at recreation and at the table. Let your life be ever concentrated on God. Walk in and with God. If your days are filled with pious aspirations, no amount of external labors or contact with the world will leave their impression. You will use the world as though you used it not, for "your conversation will be in Heaven,"[212] as the apostle suggests.

Walking in the presence of God is one of the fundamental exercises of the spiritual life, for it applies to all your actions and renders them holy and supernatural. It is practically impossible to lead an interior life without it. And if neglected, it can scarcely be supplied by any other means. It is one of the best ways of turning your actions into prayer and fulfilling the Lord's wish to "pray always."

[212] Cf. Phil. 3:20.

Part Five

∞

Let prayer permeate your life

Chapter Twenty-One

Reap the benefits of prayer

One of the best incentives to prayer is a careful consideration of the many benefits of prayer-life. St. Bernard seems to have summarized the benefits in these words: "Prayer is a wine which makes glad the heart of man. . . . It moistens the dry soil of the conscience; it brings about the perfect absorption of the food of good actions and distributes them into all the members of the soul, strengthening faith, giving vigor to hope, rendering charity active and yet well-ordered, and shedding an unction over the whole character."

If you are earnest about saving your soul, and if you realize what influence prayer has on the salvation of your soul, you will appreciate prayer and practice it constantly. Thus your prayer-life will grow, and only God knows the full extent of its benefits upon your soul.

∝

Prayer allows you to
share in God's divine life

God made us to know, love, and serve Him in this world, and to be happy with Him in the next. The reason we often neglect prayer is because we lose sight of our main duty in life: this union with God.

The supernatural life of your soul is measured by its union with God in faith and love, because God is the Author and Source of all holiness. But your soul is put in direct contact with God's divine life in the sacraments and prayer. Hence, prayer, as well as the frequent reception of the sacraments, is a necessary means to union with God. St. Augustine wrote, "The best — that is, the most perfect — man, is not he who, having reached a certain degree of perfection, halts there, but rather is he who ever tends to God, our unchangeable Life, with the most ardent yearning of his heart, and who ever unites himself with God more and more closely."

There is a hunger in everyone's heart for happiness, and prayer can satisfy this hunger. There is a yearning in everyone's heart for love, and prayer can bring the thirsting soul very close to the source of true love. When a person seeks God, God discloses Himself to the soul in prayer. Even in the midst of the business of daily life, there develops in the one who prays a tendency to seek God within himself and to speak to Him very often in holy intimacy. Prayer is loving familiarity with God.

St. Maximus the Confessor,[213] who lived in the seventh century, wrote, "All the virtues assist the soul to attain to a burning love of God, but, above all, pure prayer. By means of it, the soul escapes completely from the midst of creatures, carried to God, as it were, on wings."

---

[213] St. Maximus the Confessor (c. 580-662), Greek theologian and ascetic writer.

The movement of your soul toward God can begin and end in a split second. The greatest of all natural gifts is the will's power to seek God — and, with the aid of grace, to rise from the human level to the divine, to share the very love and life of God.

∞

Prayer increases your reverence for God

In God is to be found every good that can be imagined and in a degree that is without limit. God is all-beautiful; He is infinite love. He is the very Source of all perfection. He is eternal, the beginning and the end, "who is and who was and who is to come."[214] He is infinite wisdom; all things are known to Him. He is infinitely holy, infinitely merciful, infinitely just, and infinitely powerful. Prayer admits your soul to holy intimacy with this infinite, all-beautiful, all-sufficient, all-holy God. A profound reverence for God follows the thought of these attributes of God. You realize more than ever that God alone matters.

∞

God communicates Himself to your soul

Prayer is a heart-to-heart conversation between God and your soul, in which you express your love to Him by whom you know you are loved. The essential element of prayer is the supernatural contact of your soul with God in which you receive that divine life which is the source of all holiness. Your soul gives itself up to God, and God communicates Himself to your

[214]Rev. 1:4 (RSV).

soul. This contact is produced by the Holy Spirit through His seven gifts.[215] It is a striking thought that even though you are just a common, ordinary human being with many faults and weaknesses, the great God of Heaven not only becomes your Friend when you pray, but actually unites Himself with your soul to enrich it with His grace.

God gave you an immortal soul, and to show you how much He values it, He sent His Son to give His life to save it. The grace merited by His Son is the grace you receive when you pray. It is the divine life you had no right to possess, but which God gave you out of His infinite love and generosity. God has given you the privilege of uniting yourself with Him if only you want to talk to Him in prayer.

∞

Grace comes through prayer

Prayer is necessary because actual grace is necessary for all the acts bearing on salvation. St. Paul clearly states, "The Spirit also helps our weakness. For we do not know what we should pray for as we ought, but the Spirit Himself pleads for us with unutterable groanings."[216] This grace is offered to all, even to sinners; hence, all are able to pray.

Although the state of grace is not necessary in order to pray, it increases the value of prayer, since it makes us the friends of God and the living members of Jesus Christ. It is a truth of faith that without actual grace, we cannot obtain holiness or

---

[215] The seven gifts of the Holy Spirit are wisdom, understanding, counsel, fortitude, knowledge, piety, and fear of the Lord.
[216] Rom. 8:26.

even salvation. Actual grace is a supernatural help of God that enlightens our mind and strengthens our will to do good and to avoid evil. For instance, prayer is usually the best means of overcoming the sin of anger, because it not only gives us time to calm down and think more clearly, but also obtains actual grace — God's help — to be patient and kind.

Of yourself, no matter how you use your freedom, you can do nothing that would prepare you for conversion to God, nor can you persevere for any length of time, much less until death. Jesus said, "Without me, you can do nothing."[217]

Prayer, then, is the normal, the efficacious, and the universal means through which God wills that you obtain all actual graces. This is why Jesus insisted so frequently upon the necessity of prayer: "Ask, and it shall be given you; seek, and you shall find; knock, and it shall be opened to you. For everyone who asks receives; and he who seeks finds; and to him who knocks, it shall be opened."[218] It is as if He said, "Unless you ask, you shall not receive; unless you seek, you shall not find." He stresses this need of prayer especially to resist temptation: "Watch and pray, that you may not enter into temptation. The spirit indeed is willing, but the flesh is weak."[219]

St. Thomas says that confidence not based on prayer is presumption, for God, who is not in justice bound to grant us His grace, has not pledged Himself to give it except through prayer. God knows your spiritual needs without your making them known to Him; yet He wills that prayer be the spring

[217] John 15:5.
[218] Matt. 7:7-8 (RSV).
[219] Matt. 26:41 (RSV).

that sets in motion His loving mercy, so that you may acknowledge Him as the Author of the gifts He bestows on you.

God does not command the impossible, for He commands us to do what we can and to ask His help for what we cannot do. His grace even helps us to ask for help!

∽

Prayer prepares your soul to receive grace

The sacraments are the authentic channels of grace. They produce grace by the very fact of being applied to your soul, as long as you do not place any obstacle in the way of their action. Such obstacles would be uncharitableness, an unforgiving spirit, willful venial sin, living in the occasion of sin, and neglect of prayer. In his pastoral letter *On the Right Ordering of Christian Life*, Pope Leo XIII wrote, "As God created all things by His word, so man by prayer obtains whatever he wills. Nothing has so great a power to obtain grace for us as prayer when rightly made; for it contains the motives by which God easily allows Himself to be appeased and to incline to mercy."[220]

An increase of grace depends, at least in part, on the way you may be disposed to accept grace. But prayer prepares your soul to receive grace by putting it in the proper disposition.

As you kneel in prayer, you become more and more aware of your own nothingness. The light of God reveals to you your position before your Creator and teaches you self-knowledge. You recognize your sinfulness in the face of God's limitless holiness.

---

[220] *Exeunte Iam Anno* (December 25, 1888).

Prayer animates, perfects, and maintains the sentiments of faith, humility, confidence, and love, which together form the best disposition for your soul if it is to receive a rich share of grace. In this way, union with God in prayer makes the reception of the sacraments more fruitful.

The sacraments give a measure of grace in proportion to the dispositions of those who receive them. Prayer is most important in supplying that disposition.

Our Lord was so anxious to be united with you that He appointed prayer, besides the different sacraments, as the source of grace. Although prayer is not of itself as efficacious as the sacraments, it is no less necessary in order to obtain God's help and grace. You might compare prayer to breathing. What breathing is to the life of your body, prayer is to the supernatural life of your soul. Without breathing, the life of your body must cease; without prayer, your soul will lose grace and union with God. Neglect of prayer spells doom for your soul.

Since an increase of grace depends on your dispositions to receive it, and since prayer maintains those dispositions, pray much, so that you may receive much grace.

∞

Prayer makes you Christlike

Your most important task in life is to pattern your life according to Christ's example. If you live by His principles and depend on His help, you will have peace in your own life, and if millions of other human beings do the same, there will be peace in the whole world.

You are holy only insofar as you imitate Jesus Christ, as the heavenly Father declared at the Transfiguration: "This is my beloved Son, in whom I am well pleased; hear Him."[221] To be transformed into Jesus, you must live in close union with Him.

Jesus Christ is your hope. He said, "No man comes to the Father but through me."[222] Jesus Christ has merited grace through His life and sacred Passion. Through the sacraments and through prayer, the grace of Christ is communicated to your soul. As His life flows into your soul, the life of sin disappears. Your soul grows more and more in a new life, and in the words of St. Paul, you become "a new creature."[223]

You can now kneel in prayer clothed with the merits of Christ, the well-beloved Son of God. You are inflamed with the love of His Sacred Heart. Looking upon you, the Father sees that you have become like Jesus; you have become another well-beloved child.

∞

Life with Jesus is impossible without prayer

Prayer enlightens your mind and enkindles your heart with love to make your soul pliable. Only then can the Holy Spirit mold it by His grace, take away its defects, and give it the virtues of Jesus Christ. This is the effect of actual grace received through prayer. Your life with Jesus is developed in the measure in which Jesus is the Light of your mind, the Love ruling all the affections of your heart, the Strength in your trials and work, and the Food of that life of grace which makes you share even the life of God.

[221] Matt. 17:5.
[222] John 14:6.
[223] 2 Cor. 5:17; Gal. 6:15.

After you have been brought into intimate contact with Jesus through prayer, you come forth cleansed and purified, so that Christ reigns supreme in your soul. Through prayer, you have the power of being made spiritually beautiful in the sight of God with the beauty of Christ, of loving the Father with Christ's love, of burning with zeal for souls as Christ's heart burned, of hating sin with the same hatred that Jesus showed toward it.

An outstanding example of this transformation into Christ is St. Paul. On the road to Damascus, where he was going to continue his persecutions against the Christians, he was struck blind. On arriving in Damascus, there followed in dramatic sequence his sudden conversion, the cure of his blindness by the disciple Ananias, and his baptism. Paul accepted eagerly the commission to preach the Gospel of Christ, but he felt his unworthiness and withdrew from the world to spend three years in Arabia in meditation and prayer before beginning his apostolate. From the moment of his return, he never paused in his labors. In his prolonged prayer-life, Paul's soul became more like that of His Master. His work for souls was charity in action, for the inner spring that drove his soul to action was the overflowing of the charity of Christ, which he acquired through prayer.

In his life, as in the lives of all the saints, prayer and action were molded together in perfect harmony. St. Paul's life became the most extraordinary career of preaching, writing, and Church-founding of which we have record. Although he himself was forever pressing onward, his letters often invoked a spirit of quiet prayer and mediation, as when he ends his letter to the Philippians: "Whatever is true, whatever is honorable, whatever is just, whatever is pure, whatever is lovely, whatever is gracious, if there is any excellence, if there is anything worthy of praise, think about these things";[224] and, "Have this mind in you which was also in Christ Jesus."[225] He urged his Christians to "pray without ceasing,"[226] as he, indeed, endeavored to do. It was this prayer that changed him more and more into Christ, so that he could say, "It is no longer I who live, but Christ who lives in me."[227]

Through prayer, you will keep Jesus before you as the Model you must imitate, for it is necessary for you to become like Jesus if you wish to be pleasing to God. Through frequent Holy Communion and prayer, He will make you "another Christ" by the power of His grace, so that the heavenly Father may also say of you, "This is my beloved son, in whom I am well pleased."

∞

Prayer gives spiritual strength

Through prayer, the strength of divine grace penetrates your soul, like the sap flowing from the trunk into the branches of a tree. Prayer enlightens your mind by fixing it more firmly in faith. It supplies supernatural energy for your will so that, although weak by nature, you become capable of heroic virtue when aided by the grace of God. Thus, your mind and your will are strengthened by the life of prayer, because love is

---

[224] Phil. 4:8 (RSV).
[225] Phil. 2:5 (RSV).
[226] 1 Thess. 5:16 (RSV).
[227] Gal. 2:20 (RSV).

strengthened. Jesus purifies this love and increases it, so that, filled with such love, you can dedicate your whole being to the glory of God and the salvation of souls, especially your own.

You need this spiritual strength in order to be courageous enough to undertake difficult tasks and to face problems without fear. You need spiritual strength to be patient in suffering.

You need spiritual strength to resist temptations and to be generous in fighting vice and in working hard to acquire virtue. Do not depend on your natural ability, which may be helpful but not adequate. Acknowledge your weakness, and put your faith in the power of God, who will give you strength if you pray so that you can exclaim with St. Paul, "When I am weak, then I am strong."[228]

When you are attempting a task — big or small — stop for a moment and pray, in all humility, for God's help. God is your strength, but that strength is not yours until you ask Him to help you. Only His strength joined with yours will carry you through difficulties that you could never master alone.

Prayer is a protection against the dangers arising from your human weakness and from your contact with the world. The Lord's advice to his disciples in the Garden of Olives still holds: "Watch and pray, that you may not enter into temptation. The spirit indeed is willing, but the flesh is weak."[229]

Down through the centuries, souls have found strength to remain true to God in spite of the many temptations of the world, the flesh, and the Devil. Others have found strength in prayer to give up their sinful ways.

[228] 2 Cor. 12:10 (RSV).
[229] Matt. 26:41 (RSV).

Prayer is as necessary to obtain grace and to persevere in grace as a pipeline from a reservoir is for a city's water supply, or a system of wiring connecting generators in a city's power plant is for electrical illumination. Destroy the pipeline, and there will be a shortage of water. Cut the current-carrying wires, and there will be darkness. Neglect prayer, and there will be spiritual disaster. Every lapse from grace, every case of eternal damnation, can be traced back to the neglect of or the bad performance of prayer.

Pray constantly that you may have God's strength to fight sin, practice virtue, bear your daily cross, and save your soul.

⨷

Prayer is a shield against discouragement

The true prayerful spirit is of its nature humble. It springs from the consciousness of its own impotence coupled with the firm belief that with God, it can do all things. St. Paul expressed it thus: "Not that we are sufficient of ourselves to think anything, as from ourselves, but our sufficiency is from God."[230] God must find a way: thus thinks and speaks the man of the interior spirit. And it is in this spirit that his work is carried on. Instead of placing all reliance upon human counsel and assistance, every labor, undertaking, and cross is preceded by a humble prayer to God: "O God, come to my assistance!"[231] And he continues, "Our help is in the name of the Lord!"[232] God will accomplish it and make it successful. Thus, he shrinks

---

[230] 2 Cor. 3:5.
[231] Ps. 69:2 (RSV = Ps. 70:1).
[232] Ps. 123:8 (RSV = Ps. 124:8).

from no task, no difficulty, no cross. Again, with Paul, he exclaims, "I can do all things in him who strengthens me!"[233]

But God, who, as the psalmist says, "is nigh unto all them that call upon Him,"[234] blesses the labors of His faithful, often with unsuspected fruits. In imitation of His Master, he finds strength in prayer. Did He not, in crucial moments, withdraw Himself into the world of the interior spirit, thus to speak intimately with His heavenly Father? Before He chose His Apostles, He meditated throughout the night. Before calling the dead to life, before the institution of the Blessed Sacrament, before His Passion, He held intimate communion with His Father — not merely interiorly, but as the Scriptures have it, by raising His eyes to Heaven.[235]

If prayer is to be a shield against discouragement, you must lift your spirit from the sordid earth toward God, particularly in important matters and as an introduction to busy times. If you wish to achieve the spirit of the interior life of prayer, this intimate conversing with God will be not only a loving concern and care, but a deep-seated necessity and joy.

In looking for success in your work, you may make the mistake of depending too much on yourself and too little on God. By doing things not out of love for God but for yourself, you will reach the point of making yourself the principle and end of all your activity. God may allow a direct attack by the Devil or the world or your own personal inclinations to evil to strike at your work or even at your person, and the result is failure

[233] Phil. 4:13 (RSV).
[234] Ps. 144:18 (RSV = Ps. 145:18).
[235] John 11:41.

followed by sadness and depression. Then the Devil begins to use his most valuable tool: discouragement.

One of the most effective protections against discouragement is the comforting conviction that if you pray, you do not work alone. Christ is ever with you. You are His instrument no matter how defective you are.

The secret of humble triumph in the midst of defeat is union with our Lord through love and prayer and an unshaken confidence in His power. If storms come on, it should matter little who caused them. You have nothing to fear as long as you have worked only with Jesus and for Jesus. He will restore your peace and security. Instead of acting alone, begin your work again with Jesus, by Him, and in Him. A new raising of your heart to God in prayer will be the first result of this trial. Instead of being crushed by failure, your soul will come forth refreshed by prayer and more determined to do God's will.

One of the most precious gifts of the Lord to His loved ones is that daily growing confidence in His goodness and mercy. From the interior life in God, there grows an exceedingly wonderful familiarity with Him and a kind of childlike candor toward Him. Although others may cling to their rigoristic views and verdicts, the man of prayer knows how, if necessary, to utter with the divinely inspired singer: "Praise the Lord, for He is good, for His mercy endureth forever."[236] Although others see sin everywhere — and everywhere the Judge and the Avenger — the man of prayer praises the God of mercy and the God of all consolation, who for us men and for our salvation came down from Heaven; who mingled with sinners and

[236] Ps. 135:1 (RSV = Ps. 136:1).

even ate with them. This tender reliance upon the goodness of God accompanies him to the very portals of death, which he greets, like Francis of Assisi,[237] as a brother to accompany him.

∽

Through prayer, you make
the riches of Christ your own

The infinite wealth of the Sacred Heart enriches your poverty. Although you are a sinner, Christ is sinless and He is your Friend. Although you are weak, Christ is strong. Although you are cold, the fire of Christ's love will inflame you, the mercy of Christ's Heart will embrace you, and the patience of Christ's Heart will encourage you to continue on a virtuous way of life.

You will suffer, of course, but prayer will help to convince you that trials, generously undergone, increase your progress in virtue and give God greater glory. This conviction supported by prayer will be enough to keep you from discouragement. Besides, God may want from you only the seeds of success; others will come who will reap a plentiful harvest, but God knows the cause and will reward accordingly. Your life may be like that of Jesus. He was the author of the success of His Apostles after Pentecost, but He had to sow the seed during the course of His public life by work, suffering, and prayer.

The strength you derive from your faith in God gives you the courage to have confidence in yourself. Someone has put it this way: "When I pray, I pray as if everything depended

---

[237] St. Francis of Assisi (c. 1182-1226), founder of the Franciscan Order.

upon God. And when I work, I work as if everything depended upon me." But Scripture says, "The beginning of the pride of man is to fall off from God."[238]

Prayer strengthens you in your state of resignation to God's will. You will cheerfully submit all your plans and your hopes to the loving Providence of God, who often makes greater use of defeats than of triumphs for the good of souls. Resignation will in no way lessen your zeal in your work. You will work as if God worked with you — and He really does, when you pray.

∞

Prayer gives you joy and consolation

True joy is to be found in God, and prayer unites your soul with God.

St. Francis of Assisi was walking in the woods with good Brother Juniper, who said, "How happy the birds in the air, the animals in the grass, and the fish in the brook are! Father Francis, why is it that men are not as happy as that?" "Well, Brother, it is this way," answered the saint, "the birds, the animals, and the fish are made for this world; that is why they are so happy. Men are not made for this world; that is why they cannot be happy here."

Nothing on earth can really satisfy this longing for happiness. St. Francis in his youth tried to find happiness in the riches and pleasures of this world. He left these things in order that he might find true happiness in God in this world and especially in the next. God alone is the true source of joy. When you pray, you unite yourself with this source and share in the

[238] Ecclus. 10:14.

joy of God Himself, who communicates it to you. You were made for God; your happiness is to be sought in Him alone. This is why prayer should be a kind of "second nature" to you.

• *Prayer gives you joy in sacrifice.* Your life surely has its share of suffering and toil. If you do not have the conviction of being loved by God, if you fail to bear your cross for the love of God, and if you give way to sadness rather than to prayer, how miserable your life will be! Frequent Communion and earnest prayer will make your love grow greater, and you will be more generous in sacrificing yourself for the most important work of saving your soul. An ardent love for God is alone capable of brightening your life, for love possesses the secret of gladdening the heart even in the midst of great sorrows and crushing weariness.

Blessed peace in God, blessed sufficiency in God, blessed joy in God, blessed rest in God — these are the precious fruits of an interior life of union with God. Interior souls know the true meaning of the words: "Taste and see that the Lord is sweet!"[239] They realize full well the truth of the psalmist's exclamation: "But it is good for me to adhere to my God, to put my hope in the Lord God."[240]

The diaries and writings of the saints tell the story of the peace and joy they felt in serving God, even in the midst of the greatest trials. They act on the motto "Leave all, and you will find all," and they become rich

[239] Ps. 33:9 (RSV = Ps. 34:8).
[240] Ps. 72:28 (RSV = Ps. 73:28).

and free, ever rejoicing in God, who permits some of the joys of Heaven to descend upon their souls. They never fear the tasks and burdens of the day, or even its sorrows and anguishes. For in these very sorrows they find God and, in nearness to God, His riches of joy and consolation.

"My soul magnifies the Lord, and my spirit rejoices in God my Savior."[241] Thus spoke the Mother of God, expressing her joy and gratitude because of God's infinite condescension to all mankind — and to her in particular.

Peace and joy are the rewards of the interior life of prayer, for they are specifically characterized by the Apostle as the fruits of the Spirit.[242] Thus it is that interior souls bear the mark of joy on their faces, and they spread its blessings wherever they go. They find joy and peace in everything: walks through the countryside, elevating music, the starry heavens, the sight of an innocent child, and all life's contacts and experience. God shines forth in all things for them; they are constantly using creatures as stepping stones to the majesty of the Creator. Your soul's demands for more joy can be satisfied only by a greater devotion to the interior life of prayer.

It was St. Paul's love inspired by prayer that led him to exclaim, "I overflow with joy in all our troubles."[243]

[241] Luke 1:46-47 (RSV).
[242] Gal. 5:22.
[243] 2 Cor. 7:4.

St. John Vianney,[244] the Curé of Ars, had his way of expressing this effect of prayer: "The life of prayer: this is real happiness here below. O beautiful life, beautiful union of the soul with our Lord. Eternity will not be long enough to understand this happiness. . . . Interior life is a bath of love into which the soul plunges. . . . It is, as it were, drowned in love. God holds the interior soul as a mother holds the head of her child in her hand to cover him with kisses and caresses."

• *Joy is the result of a life of prayer.* But this joy is, above all, spiritual. God does not always allow this inward joy to react upon your feelings. Do not be discouraged if you remain in a state of dryness even during prayer. Deep down in your soul, there will be peace. Christ acts silently but surely in the depths of your soul in order to change it into Himself. The more earnestly you pray, the more will you understand how sweet the Lord really is.

Jesus encouraged you to pray for this spiritual joy: "Ask and you shall receive, that your joy may be full."[245] To ask in the name of Jesus is to ask for what is useful to your salvation, while remaining united to Jesus by faith and love as a living member of His Mystical Body. If you give yourself faithfully to prayer, you will be detached more and more from created things, with the result that you will enter more fully into the life of God. This is a foretaste of an eternal union with Him in Heaven, for

---

[244] St. John Vianney (1786-1859), patron saint of parish priests.
[245] John 16:24.

your inward joy is made perfect little by little. It will reach its fullness one day in heavenly bliss.

The moments of union with Jesus during prayer may be counted as the happiest of your life. Let this spiritual joy fill each hour of the day's work. Let this joy radiate toward other souls, so that they may be filled with some of your happiness.

Spiritual joy is one of the characteristics of a saint. The saints sought this joy at its source — union with God in prayer! St. John Chrysostom wrote, "Reflect what great happiness is bestowed upon you, what glory is given to you — namely, to converse in your prayers with God, to join in colloquy with Christ, and to beg for what you wish or desire."

• *Prayer is the source of consolation in all the sufferings of your life.* God will never fail you, if you turn to Him in prayer, either in the Blessed Sacrament or in the temple of your own heart, where He dwells by grace.

When crosses come, many of us complain instead of praying. Instead of complaining, turn to God in prayer, receive the sacraments, and be more earnest about spiritual things. Use your religion to obtain the strength you need to accept your crosses in life.

Prayer is your greatest consolation in the sufferings of life because prayer unites you with the God of consolation. Especially at the hour of death, you will find true consolation in prayer.

How beautiful are the words of the psalmist: "I am always with thee. Thou hast held me by Thy right hand;

and by Thy will Thou hast conducted me, and with Thy glory Thou hast received me. For what have I in Heaven? And besides Thee, what do I desire upon earth? For Thee my flesh and my heart hath fainted away: for Thou art the God of my heart, and the God that is my portion forever."[246] Such peace of spirit in the midst of suffering as fruit of the interior life of prayer should alone suffice to make you devote yourself to prayer wholeheartedly and cheerfully.

When you feel the burdens of your daily life pressing upon you, listen to the tender appeal of Christ's Sacred Heart: "Come to me, all you who labor and are burdened, and I will give you rest."[247] True consolation comes from divine love. You cannot rest in God more surely than at Holy Communion and prayer, because then you are united in divine love with God, your greatest and most lovable Good, as St. Augustine wrote: "Our hearts were made for Thee, O Lord, and they are restless until they rest in Thee."

⁓

Love gives value to your actions

Your holiness depends upon the way you perform your actions. The greater the love with which you do things, the more pleasing are these actions in the sight of God.

But you cannot perform these actions out of love consistently and regularly unless you live a life of prayer. Prayer fills

[246] Ps. 72:23-26 (RSV = Ps. 73:23-26).
[247] Matt. 11:28.

your heart with God's love, and that love prompts you to action penetrated with the love of God. Every moment of your work will give you a chance to show your charity. You will manage to carry out everything with greater purity of intention. In this way, each of your actions will be filled daily with the stamp of God's grace and the character of the holiness of Jesus Christ.

How many a prayerful mother performs her daily tasks as an act of love for God and thereby makes her whole life a prayer! She prays in her innermost soul without knowing it as long as she remains faithful to the way laid down by the divine will in the spirit of loving obedience. As St. John of the Cross wrote, "The road to Heaven is narrow. He who would walk on it with ease must divest himself of all things and lean upon the Cross for support; that is, he must be resolved to suffer all things for the love of God."

A mother, without tiring her mind, makes many acts of love. These acts uplift her whole life and give it fresh value. That is the true way to acquire the Christian virtues, for these come only from the power of Christ — imparted to us through prayer — for He is the fullness from which we all have received.

∞

Prayer and action go together
Your prayer-life and active life are important to each other. They do not exclude each other; rather, they go together, call for each other's help, and complement each other. If one of them is to get a larger share of attention than the other, it is prayer-life, which is the more perfect and the more necessary.

Prayer in your life is what the heart is in the human body. The heart gives life and strength to the members of the body by the blood that it sends to them.

A life of union with God in prayer makes your work more spiritual and gives it a kind of supernatural character. Prayer alone will give your activity real usefulness, for it will be worthwhile only insofar as God has a share in it. Your prayer-life puts God into everything you do.

The sacramentals of the Church are an excellent means of associating our prayer-life with our active life. The chief benefits obtained by the use of sacramentals are actual graces, the forgiveness of venial sins, the remission of temporal punishment, health of body and material blessing, and protection from evil spirits. The chief kinds of sacramentals are blessings given by priests and bishops, as well as blessed objects of devotion, such as holy water, candles, ashes, palms, crucifixes, medals, rosaries, scapulars, and images of our Lord, of our Lady, and of the saints. The Church wants us to make use of the sacramentals with faith and devotion, and this necessarily includes prayer.

Good works should be the overflow of your interior life of prayer. You must share in the divine life of grace first and be filled with it before you can be the instrument whereby others receive it. What great power you will have in speaking to your children about prayer if your children see you frequently conversing with God. Converts are won and souls inspired less by long and frequent discussions, than by good example.

St. Teresa said, "A saintly man does more real good to souls than a great number of others who are learned and better gifted."

∞

Christ gives life to your soul

Christ is the source of the life of your soul, so you must abide in Him. By means of the sacraments and prayer, you absorb His divine life, and being filled with it, you enable others to share its fruits. Your prayer-life must be the branch filled with life-giving sap, of which your good works are but the flowers.

Prayer leads you to a burning personal love for Jesus Christ, who said, "Without me you can do nothing." Prayer teaches you to understand how perfectly He answers the description of a true Friend — a Friend who redeemed you, enriched your souls with His grace, clothed you with His merits in the sight of the Father, and promised you Heaven as a reward for your loyalty to Him. And each time you rejected all this by rebelling against God by sin, He sought you like a Good Shepherd, granted you His pardon, and again reinstated you in His grace, almost as if you were in some way necessary to God's happiness.

Our Lord taught St. Gertrude[248] to turn often toward the crucifix in prayer and imagine Him to be speaking from it: "See how for love of you I have been fastened to the Cross, despised, naked, torn; my body covered with wounds and my bones dislocated. Yet my Heart is so eager for your love that, if it were necessary for your salvation, I would suffer again, for you alone, all that I suffered for the sins of the whole world."

The saints have found in the crucifix one of the richest sources of meditation on the love of God for us.

[248] St. Gertrude (1256-c. 1302), German mystic.

Chapter Twenty-Two

Cultivate a spirit of prayer

You must not be "religious" only at Mass on Sundays, or every morning for three minutes after rising and every evening for a few minutes before going to bed.

Prayer should be the breath of your soul. Conscious of your human weakness, and trusting in God's power, goodness, and fidelity, you should constantly turn to Him in prayer. Pray in the morning when you arise, offering the day to Him and asking His blessing. Turn to Him often during the course of the day with short but fervent prayers, such as these:

Jesus, my God,
I love You above all things!

All for you,
O Sacred Heart of Jesus!

My Jesus, mercy!

Say your prayers before and after meals with reverence and gratitude, and not in a slovenly manner. Recite the rosary daily to obtain the help of the Mother of God. And, when evening comes, kneel down and ask God's pardon for the faults of

the day, thank Him for His benefits, and beg for the grace to
serve Him better tomorrow.

Pray especially in time of temptation. For it is only by the
grace of God, given in response to prayer, that you can long resist the assaults of the enemies of your soul: the world, the
flesh, and the Devil. If, however, you continue to pray, you can
be certain that you will not fall into sin.

Every day of your life, pray for the gift of final perseverance,
that the decisive moment of death may find you with the love
and the grace of God in your heart. Ask for this crowning
grace through the intercession of the Mother of God.

Outside these official exercises of piety, God is just as lovable, just as easy to talk to, and just as near. To know that is to
understand the difference between praying and possessing the
spirit of prayer, between having a kind of piety and possessing
an inward life. You cannot always be in the act of praying, but
you should always be in a state of prayer. This is what Jesus
meant when He told people "that they must always pray and
not lose heart."[249]

St. Teresa wrote, "We must withdraw in spirit far from all
external things and come inwardly nearer to God; even in our
daily occupations we must retire within ourselves, were it only
for a moment — in short, we should gradually accustom ourselves to converse quietly with Him."

And St. Patrick,[250] in his Confessions, wrote, "In a single day,
I have prayed as many as a hundred times, and in the night almost as often."

---

[249] Luke 18:1.
[250] St. Patrick (c. 390-c. 460), patron saint and apostle of Ireland.

The spirit of prayer — or habitual prayer — may be described as a lasting and sympathetic awareness of God's presence. Your soul dwells in an atmosphere of recollectedness, sensing God's presence as you might sense the presence of another who is very ill while you go about your duties. Whether you call it sensing the presence of God, or silent prayer, it is one of God's greatest gifts to your soul.

Endeavor to acquire the spirit of prayer, which is composed of three elements:

• *A great esteem for prayer*, a vivid realization of the sublimity and excellence of prayer in itself: prayer is the best and noblest activity of which you are capable, because it is conversation with God.

• *The conviction of the absolute need for prayer* for your spiritual life, your spiritual progress, and your soul's very salvation: prayer is an indispensable and unique means of grace and perfection.

• *Absolute confidence in the power of prayer:* with prayer, you can do all things, because God has promised you all things. This confidence consists in a firm conviction that there is nothing you cannot accomplish and obtain by good and persevering prayer. Of course, the prayer must be in conformity with the claims of reason and conscience and subject to the will of God, who is all-good and all-knowing.

The spirit of prayer is one of the most precious graces in the spiritual life — indeed, the chief of all graces, the beginning and fulfillment of all good. So long as it lives within you, you will be grounded and rooted in God and in all that is good, and all within you can be restored and turned to good. Without it, your whole spiritual life is unreliable.

A spirit of prayer must pervade and sanctify everything you do. Even in the most absorbing occupations, try to preserve this spirit. You will do so if you fulfill these two conditions: that you habitually live the life of prayer; and that you do not permit your activity to do away with the life of prayer. This may happen if you withdraw your activity from the influence of our Lord.

The more your heart is united to our Lord in prayer, the more it shares in the dominating qualities of the divine and human Heart of the Redeemer. Your life of prayer will radiate faith, hope, charity, humility, prudence, self-sacrifice, firmness and gentleness — and all these virtues will influence every action of your life. Thus the spirit of prayer will counteract the obstacles to prayer: pride, selfishness, and sin. The spirit of prayer will necessarily draw down the blessing of God upon your work. That blessing will influence your neighbor, and thus God will be glorified through your prayerful life. Without a life of prayer, you accomplish little more than nothing, for it is altogether certain that no good work can be carried on without the grace of God.

∾

Learn how to develop
a spirit of prayer

If you really want to make Jesus the life of all your works, make definite resolutions for intensifying your interior life and act on the following principles:

• *Look at life as it really is,* remembering that this world will pass away, while the next is eternal and that your greatest duty is to give glory to God and to save your soul.

• *Love God above all things* and find delight in Him alone, and for His sake love your neighbor and all God's creatures.

• *See the hands of God's Providence in all that happens,* and, with confidence, abandon yourself to His loving guidance.

• *Love the Blessed Virgin Mary* sincerely as your Mother and model. Pray the rosary daily.

• *Hate sin,* even venial sin, as the world's greatest evil, and, thus, avoid every occasion that will lead you into it. If you should fall through human weakness, be sincerely sorry and penitent, and return to an even more intimate friendship with God through a good confession. Receive the Sacrament of Penance regularly.

• *Shun the spirit of the world,* despise its interests and opinions, and never conform to its ways.

• *Regard Holy Mass, Holy Communion, visits to the Blessed Sacrament, and liturgical functions as the most fruitful sources of your interior life,* and, if you can, go to Mass and receive Communion daily.

• *Perform your work for the love of God,* rather than through mere natural energy and self-love.

♦ *Devote a definite time each day to mental and vocal prayer.* Do not have confidence only in your own efforts, but truly depend on God, for God is the principal agent; you are only His instrument. Therefore, work hard, as if everything depended on you; but pray harder, knowing that everything really depends upon God.

♦ *Do not remain engaged for too long in excessive work* that would leave your soul in a state of estrangement from God or render it difficult for you to raise your thoughts to God occasionally.

♦ *Try to remain recollected and under the influence of God's grace during your work*, even if it is only by a short, yet sure, directing of your mind to Him, a simple loving movement of your heart toward Him, or by using some brief, spontaneous prayer. Be firmly convinced that you can do nothing more important for your own soul and those of others — for God's glory and for the good of the Church — than to cultivate your interior life through the sacraments, prayer, and good works, remembering the Savior's words: "Abide in me, and I in you. As the branch cannot bear fruit of itself unless it abide in the vine, so neither can you unless you abide in me."[251]

∞

Through prayer, you will find God

The example of Christ at Nazareth and during His public life emphasizes the importance of the spirit of prayer. It is in

[251] John 15:4-5.

direct contrast to modern rush and activity that allows no time for the soul to rest in God. Christ's standards are very different from those of the world. The world would consider His thirty years of hidden life in Nazareth a waste of time.

The work of the sanctification of an individual soul is of more importance in the eyes of God than the material welfare of the nation. It is not so much *what* you do that matters as *why* you do it. It is not so much what you *do* as what you *become* that is of value in God's eyes. His plan for your soul is that it become transformed interiorly. And all your soul's sanctification comes from contact with Christ; and contact with Christ is made by prayer. Prayer is the life of true achievement, the instrument best fitted to do God's work in your soul.

If you are faithful in speaking with God and in listening to what the Holy Spirit brings to your mind, your soul will constantly express itself in acts of faith, hope, love, confidence, repentance, and submission to the will of God. It will move in an atmosphere conducive to maintaining union with God. Prayer will become the breath, the life of your soul. Eventually prayer will develop into a state, and your soul will be able to find God at will, even in the midst of many occupations. The moments in the day that you consecrate exclusively to the formal exercise of prayer will be only the intensifying of this state in which your soul remains habitually but gently united to God, speaking to Him interiorly and listening to His voice.

If you seek God with your whole heart because you love Him with your whole heart, you will never seek in vain. For, more lovingly than you can realize, God is seeking you. You must remove the obstacles that you have put in the way of God's finding your soul. The more you find God, through prayer, so much the more fervently will you seek Him. You will be living in the true spirit of prayer. You will find God in your joys and in your sorrows; you will see Him in your dearest friends as well as in your enemies. If you love God, you will find Him in every circumstance of life, because your heart is in Heaven. Yours will be a peace and joy that no man can take from you! And this is the glorious aim of prayer in your life — the possession of God!

Lawrence G. Lovasik

(1913-1986)

"Life is short, and we must all give account of it on the Day of Judgment," said Fr. Lawrence Lovasik. "I am in earnest about using the time allotted to me by God on this earth to the best advantage in carrying out the ideal of my life — to make God more known and loved through my writings."[252]

The oldest of eight children, Lawrence Lovasik was born of Slovak parents in the steel-industry town of Tarentum, Pennsylvania. He was accepted into the Sacred Heart Mission Seminary in Girard, Pennsylvania, at the age of twelve and, after thirteen years of study and training, was ordained to the priesthood at St. Mary's Mission Seminary in Techny, Illinois, in 1938. Fr. Lovasik studied further at Rome's Gregorian Papal University, spent three years as a teacher and prefect of seminarians, and went on to do missionary work in America's coal and steel regions. In 1955, he founded the Sisters of the Divine Spirit, an American religious congregation of home and foreign

---

[252] Walter Romig, *The Book of Catholic Authors*, 5th ser. (Grosse Pointe, Michigan: Walter Romig and Company, 1943), 181.

missionaries whose services included teaching in schools and in catechetical classes, visiting homes, and assisting in social work.

Fr. Lovasik devoted much of his time to giving missions and retreats. These experiences and that of his earlier missionary work acquainted him with the spiritual needs, personal and family problems, and individual plans and longings of God's people, and he yearned to help them. Christ's exhortation to His first priests — "Go, and make disciples of all nations"[253] — was his inspiration. "I wanted to reach the hearts of people," he said, "but my voice could be heard only by those to whom I was able to preach."[254] Writing, he found, was his way to preach God's love and truth to the many, and it was his personal love for Christ, for the Blessed Mother, and for all immortal souls that drove him to dedicate as much time as possible to this talent.

Prayer and the Holy Eucharist are the emphases of many of the several books and more than fifty pamphlets that Fr. Lovasik wrote. His style is simple, sincere, and highly practical. He combines his vision of the transforming power of holiness and his compassionate understanding of man's desires and weaknesses to offer sound spiritual direction that motivates and inspires his readers, leads them step by step toward holiness, warns them against spiritual and temporal pitfalls, and guides them back to the right path when they go astray. Fr. Lovasik's wisdom not only reveals the often overlooked strength of holiness, but also continues to make real his life's ideal — to make God more known and loved.

[253] Matt. 28:19.
[254] Romig, The Book of Catholic Authors, 180.

Sophia Institute

Sophia Institute is a nonprofit institution that seeks to nurture the spiritual, moral, and cultural life of souls and to spread the Gospel of Christ in conformity with the authentic teachings of the Roman Catholic Church.

Sophia Institute Press fulfills this mission by offering translations, reprints, and new publications that afford readers a rich source of the enduring wisdom of mankind.

Sophia Institute also operates two popular online Catholic resources: CrisisMagazine.com and CatholicExchange.com.

Crisis Magazine provides insightful cultural analysis that arms readers with the arguments necessary for navigating the ideological and theological minefields of the day. *Catholic Exchange* provides world news from a Catholic perspective as well as daily devotionals and articles that will help you to grow in holiness and live a life consistent with the teachings of the Church.

In 2013, Sophia Institute launched Sophia Institute for Teachers to renew and rebuild Catholic culture through service to Catholic education. With the goal of nurturing the spiritual, moral, and cultural life of souls, and an abiding respect for the role and work of teachers, we strive to provide materials and programs that are at once enlightening to the mind and ennobling to the heart; faithful and complete, as well as useful and practical.

Sophia Institute gratefully recognizes the Solidarity Association for preserving and encouraging the growth of our apostolate over the course of many years. Without their generous and timely support, this book would not be in your hands.

www.SophiaInstitute.com
www.CatholicExchange.com
www.CrisisMagazine.com
www.SophiaInstituteforTeachers.org

Sophia Institute Press® is a registered trademark of Sophia Institute.
Sophia Institute is a tax-exempt institution as defined by the
Internal Revenue Code, Section 501(c)(3). Tax I.D. 22-2548708.